MONEY, ECONOMICS, AND FINANCE: DEVELOPMENTS, ANALYSES AND RESEARCH



# FEDERAL CREDIT

# CONCEPTS, BUDGETARY TREATMENT, AND REFORM PROPOSALS

# MONEY, ECONOMICS, AND FINANCE: DEVELOPMENTS, ANALYSES AND RESEARCH

Additional books in this series can be found on Nova's website under the Series tab.

Additional E-books in this series can be found on Nova's website under the E-book tab.

# FINANCIAL INSTITUTIONS AND SERVICES

Additional books in this series can be found on Nova's website under the Series tab.

Additional E-books in this series can be found on Nova's website under the E-book tab.

MONEY, ECONOMICS, AND FINANCE:
DEVELOPMENTS, ANALYSES AND RESEARCH

# FEDERAL CREDIT

# CONCEPTS, BUDGETARY TREATMENT, AND REFORM PROPOSALS

ETHAN A. KELLY
EDITOR

*New York*

For permission to use material from this book please contact us:
Telephone 631-231-7269; Fax 631-231-8175
Web Site: http://www.novapublishers.com



**Library of Congress Cataloging-in-Publication Data**

ISBN: 978-1-62417-553-4

*Published by Nova Science Publishers, Inc. † New York*

# CONTENTS

# PREFACE

The U.S. government uses federal credit (direct loans and loan guarantees) to allocate capital to a range of areas including home ownership, student loans, small business, agriculture, and energy. A direct loan is "a disbursement of funds by the government to a nonfederal borrower under a contract that requires the repayment of such funds with or without interest." A loan guarantee is "a pledge with respect to the payment of all or part of the principal or interest on any debt obligation of a non-federal borrower to a non-federal lender." At the end of FY2011, outstanding federal direct loans totaled $838 billion and outstanding guaranteed loans totaled $2,017 billion. This book describes the concepts, budgetary treatment and reform proposals of federal credit.

Chapter 1 – The U.S. government uses federal credit (direct loans and loan guarantees) to allocate financial capital to a range of areas, including home ownership, higher education, small business, agriculture, and energy. At the end of FY2011, outstanding federal credit totaled $2.9 trillion. This report explains the budgetary treatment of federal credit, examines proposed reforms, and describes relevant bills introduced in the 112th Congress.

Title V of the Omnibus Budget Reconciliation Act of 1990 (P.L. 101-508), the Federal Credit Reform Act of 1990 or FCRA, changed how the unified budget reports the cost of federal credit activities (i.e., federal direct loans and loan guarantees) to an accrual basis beginning in 1992. Before FY1992, for a given fiscal year, the budgetary cost of a new direct loan or loan guarantee was the net cash flow for that fiscal year. This cash flow measure did not accurately reflect the cost of a loan or loan guarantee, which is its subsidy cost over the entire life of the loan or loan guarantee, that is, its accrual cost. Beginning with FY1992, FCRA required that the reported budgetary cost of a credit program equal the estimated subsidy costs at the time the credit is provided. The FCRA defines the subsidy cost as "the estimated long-term cost to the government of a direct loan or a loan guarantee, calculated on a net present value basis, excluding administrative costs." This arguably places the cost of federal credit programs on a budgetary basis equivalent to other federal outlays. Because the subsidy costs of discretionary credit programs (such as the business loan programs of the Small Business Administration and the loan guarantee programs of the Export-Import Bank) are now provided through appropriations acts, this change meant that discretionary credit programs must compete with other discretionary programs on an equal basis. In contrast, funding for most mandatory credit programs (generally entitlement programs) is provided by permanent appropriations. The director of the Office of Management and Budget (OMB) is responsible for coordinating the estimation of subsidy costs to the federal government. Since the passage of the FCRA, federal agencies, working with OMB, have steadily improved their compliance with credit reform standards. In October 1990, the Federal Accounting Standards Advisory Board (FASAB) was established. In August 1993, this board required that agencies' accounting procedures be consistent with their budgetary procedures for their federal credit programs. On August 5, 1997, the Balanced Budget Act of 1997 (P.L. 105-33) was enacted, amending the FCRA to make technical changes, including codifying several guidelines set by OMB. Four proposals to expand credit reform have been discussed: the principles of credit reform could be applied to government-sponsored enterprises (GSEs); the principles of credit reform could be extended to federal insurance programs; the budgetary cost of capital for credit programs could be changed to include market risk; and the administrative costs of credit programs could be included in the calculation of the costs of these programs. These proposals are described in this report. In the 112th Congress, four bills have been proposed with provisions concerning the budgetary treatment of federal credit: related bills S. 1651/H.R. 3414 (Honest Budget Act); H.R. 3581 (Budget and Accounting Transparency Act of 2011); and H.R. 3844 (Honest Budget Act of 2012). H.R. 3581 was passed by the House but has not been acted on by the Senate.

Chapter 2 – Since the mid-1980s, budget experts have debated whether the best method of measuring the subsidy cost of federal credit (direct loans and loan guarantees) is the cost to the government or the fair value cost. The cost to the government would reflect the actual budget cost measured by discounting of expected cash flows associated with each program at the interest rate on risk-free Treasury securities. The measure of the cost to the government would place the cost of federal credit on the same basis as a grant or a tax expenditure; consequently, policymakers would have an incentive to use the most appropriate means to cover the cost of a government program. The fair value cost would equal the cost that the credit recipient would have had to pay to borrow on the private credit market. The fair value cost would include market risk and reflect the opportunity cost of shifting capital from the private sector to the public sector. Proponents argue that the social cost rather than the budgetary cost should be used to allocate resources between the public and private sectors. This debate has yet to be resolved. The U.S. government uses federal credit to allocate financial capital to a range of areas, including home ownership, student loans, small business, agriculture, and energy. A direct loan is a disbursement of funds by the government to a nonfederal borrower under a contract that requires the repayment of such funds with or without interest. A loan guarantee is a pledge by the federal government to repay all or part of the principal or interest on any debt obligation of a non-federal borrower to a non-federal lender. At the end of FY2011, outstanding federal direct loans totaled $838 billion and outstanding guaranteed loans totaled $2,017 billion. Before FY1992, federal credit programs were measured on an annual cash flow basis. A new federal direct loan was treated as a budget outlay in the current fiscal year, and repayments of principal and payments of interest were treated as offsetting collections (negative outlays) in the future fiscal years in which they occurred. In the year it was granted, a loan guarantee was a contingent liability, which means the federal government was only responsible for repayment in the event of a default. Congress and the executive branch debated options to convert the budgetary treatment of federal credit from cash flow accounting to accrual accounting, which would record the subsidy cost of federal credit over the entire life of a loan or loan guarantee. One of the primary decisions concerning accrual accounting was whether the subsidy cost of federal credit should be measured by the "cost to the government" or the "fair value" cost. On November 5, 1990, the President signed P.L. 101-508, 104 Stat. 1388, the Omnibus Budget Reconciliation Act of 1990 (OBRA90), which included the Federal Credit Reform Act of 1990 (FCRA). Beginning with FY1992, FCRA changed the methodology in the unified budget for measuring and reporting the cost of federal direct loans and federal loan guarantees from cash flow to accrual accounting with the cost to the government used in measuring subsidy costs. In the 112$^{th}$ Congress, six bills have been introduced that would provide for calculation of subsidy costs using fair value accounting: companion bills S. 1651/H.R. 3414 (Honest Budget Act), H.R. 3581 (Budget and Accounting did not accurately reflect the cost of a loan or loan guarantee, which is its subsidy cost over the entire life of the loan or loan guarantee, that is, its accrual cost.

Beginning with FY1992, FCRA required that the reported budgetary cost of a credit program equal the estimated subsidy costs at the time the credit is provided. The FCRA defines the subsidy cost as "the estimated long-term cost to the government of a direct loan or a loan guarantee, calculated on a net present value basis, excluding administrative costs." This arguably places the cost of federal credit programs on a budgetary basis equivalent to other federal outlays. Because the subsidy costs of discretionary credit programs (such as the business loan programs of the Small Business Administration and the loan guarantee programs of the Export-Import Bank) are now provided through appropriations acts, this change meant that discretionary credit programs must compete with other discretionary programs on an equal basis. In contrast, funding for most mandatory credit programs (generally entitlement programs) is provided by permanent appropriations. The director of the Office of Management and Budget (OMB) is responsible for coordinating the estimation of subsidy costs to the federal government.

Since the passage of the FCRA, federal agencies, working with OMB, have steadily improved their compliance with credit reform standards. In October 1990, the Federal Accounting Standards Advisory Board (FASAB) was established. In August 1993, this board required that agencies' accounting procedures be consistent with their budgetary procedures for their federal credit programs. On August 5, 1997, the Balanced Budget Act of 1997 (P.L. 105-33) was enacted, amending the FCRA to make technical changes, including codifying several guidelines set by OMB.

Four proposals to expand credit reform have been discussed: the principles of credit reform could be applied to government-sponsored enterprises (GSEs); the principles of credit reform could be extended to federal insurance programs; the budgetary cost of capital for credit programs could be changed to include market risk; and the administrative costs of credit programs could be included in the calculation of the costs of these programs. These proposals are described in this report.

In the 112$^{th}$ Congress, four bills have been proposed with provisions concerning the budgetary treatment of federal credit: related bills S. 1651/H.R. 3414 (Honest Budget Act); H.R. 3581 (Budget and Accounting Transparency Act of 2011); and H.R. 3844 (Honest Budget Act of 2012). H.R. 3581 was passed by the House but has not been acted on by the Senate.

# INTRODUCTION

The U.S. government uses federal credit (direct loans and loan guarantees) to allocate capital to a range of areas including home ownership, student loans, small business, agriculture, and energy. A direct loan is "a disbursement of funds by the government to a nonfederal borrower under a contract that requires the repayment of such funds with or without interest."[1] A loan guarantee is "a pledge with respect to the payment of all or part of the principal or interest on any debt obligation of a non-federal borrower to a non-federal lender."[2] At the end of FY2011, outstanding federal direct loans totaled $838 billion and outstanding guaranteed loans totaled $2,017 billion.[3] Thus, at the end of FY2011, outstanding federal credit totaled $2.855 trillion.

The Federal Credit Reform Act of 1990 (FCRA) in the Omnibus Budget Reconciliation Act of 1990 (P.L. 101-508, §13201; 104 Stat. 1388, 1388-610) changed the budgetary treatment of federal credit from cash-flow accounting to accrual accounting. Cash flow accounting measured the cost of a new loan or new loan guarantee by its net cash flow in the fiscal year it was provided. FCRA measures the cost of new federal credit as the net present value of cash flows over the life of the loan or loan guarantee at the time the credit is extended, using Treasury interest rates to discount the value of future cash flows.[4] Some public finance experts argue that the discount rate should be changed to include market risk.

The purposes of this report are to explain the provisions of the FCRA; examine the implementation of credit reform, including credit reform provisions of the Balanced Budget Act of 1997 (P.L. 105-33, §1011; 111 Stat. 254,692); discuss proposed modifications of credit reform; and describe proposed legislation in the 112th Congress. In order to achieve these objectives, it is necessary to initially discuss justifications for credit programs, federal credit concepts, and the budgetary treatment of federal credit before the enactment of the FCRA.[5]

Before FY1992, for a given fiscal year, the reported budgetary cost of a new loan or new loan guarantee was its net cash flow for that fiscal year. This cash flow measure did not accurately reflect the cost of a loan or loan guarantee (federal credit) to the federal government, which is its subsidy cost over the entire life of the loan or loan guarantee. Using the old cash-flow method, it was often difficult for policymakers to accurately monitor and therefore make informed decisions about federal credit. In addition, administrators at agencies could understate costs by using budgetary techniques such as generating "savings" from the fees on increased volumes of new guarantees, while ignoring the increase in expected losses, and offsetting the (cash) cost of new direct loans with current year collections from old loans.

To remedy these problems, Congress included credit reform in the Omnibus Budget Reconciliation Act of 1990 (OBRA90). The President signed OBRA90 into law on November 5, 1990. The legislation added a new title to the Congressional Budget Act, Title V, the Federal Credit Reform Act of 1990 (FCRA). Beginning with FY1992, the FCRA changed the methodology in the unified budget for measuring and reporting the cost of federal direct loans and federal loan guarantees.[6]

## JUSTIFICATIONS FOR CREDIT PROGRAMS

Federal credit programs are justified economically on two grounds: equity and efficiency.

### Equity

*Equity* concerns the distributions of income, consumption, and wealth. The distribution of income has received the most emphasis among policymakers. Because economists cannot make interpersonal comparisons of utility, the optimal distributions of income, consumption, and wealth are normative; that is, they involve value judgments. In other words, economists cannot conclude that one distribution is better than another although the degree of inequality can be measured.

Another aspect of the debate on equity concerns the appropriate method of redistribution, if desired. Some Members of Congress support redistributive programs, including credit programs, to lessen income disparities. For example, credit assistance to students from lower-income families may assist the students in pursuing higher education and thus reduce income inequality. Some critics maintain that direct subsidies can usually better target assistance to the needy than can credit programs.

### Efficiency

If an economy is productively *efficient*, it cannot produce more of one good without reducing the production of one or more other goods. For an economy to be efficient, private financial intermediaries should allocate capital to its most productive uses. Private financial intermediaries generally operate efficiently, but market imperfections exist, and these imperfections may cause an inadequate availability of credit in certain sectors of the economy. The Office of Management and Budget (OMB) states that market imperfections that can justify federal intervention "include information failures, monitoring problems, limited ability to secure resources, insufficient competition, externalities, and financial market instability."[7] "Education, for example, generates positive externalities because the general public benefits from the high productivity and good citizenship of a well-educated person."[8] Thus, arguably, credit assistance for higher education may improve economic efficiency.

## FEDERAL CREDIT CONCEPTS

Numerous terms in financial economics have specific meanings for federal budget practices. These terms include federal credit, federal credit subsidies, and the unified budget. Some of these terms are defined in the FCRA—and are summarized in the subsequent sections.

### Federal Credit

The Office of Management and Budget defines federal credit as *federal direct* loans and federal loan guarantees. The federal government extends federal credit by entering into a direct loan obligation or a loan guarantee commitment.

The FCRA defines a *direct loan* as "a disbursement of funds by the government to a nonfederal borrower under a contract that requires the repayment of such funds with or without interest" [Section 502(1)]. According to the FCRA, a *direct loan obligation* is "a binding agreement by a federal agency to make a direct loan when specified conditions are fulfilled by the borrower" [Section 502(2)]. The FCRA defines a *loan guarantee* as a "pledge with respect to the payment of all or a part of the principal or interest on any debt obligation of a non-federal borrower to a non-federal lender" [Section 502(3)]. A *loan guarantee commitment* is "a binding agreement by a federal agency to make a loan guarantee when specified conditions are fulfilled by the borrower, the lender, or any other party to the guarantee agreements" [Section 502(4)].

When either a direct loan obligation or a loan guarantee commitment is extended, the federal government determines future credit flows because the government signs a contract to provide credit. In some cases the specified conditions may not be met, and, consequently, credit will not be provided even though a contract was signed. Furthermore, there is a time lag between the signing of these contracts and the actual disbursement of a direct loan by the federal government or the actual disbursement of a guaranteed loan by a private lender. In some cases, particularly for credit for construction, credit may be disbursed by either the federal government or a private lender in increments over several fiscal years.[9]

## Federal Credit Subsidies

Federal credit recipients obtain funds on more favorable terms than they could receive from the private market. OMB has described subsidies from federal direct loans as consisting of one or more of the following:

- interest rates below commercial levels,
- longer maturities than fully private loans,
- deferral of interest,
- allowance of grace periods,
- waiver or reduction of loan fees,
- higher loan amount in relation to the value of the underlying enterprise than a fully private loan, and
- availability of funds to borrowers for purposes for which the private sector would not lend—at virtually any interest rate under virtually any repayment terms.[10]

Concerning loan guarantee subsidies, OMB stated the following:

> The recipient of a federal loan guarantee receives a subsidy because the federal government covers part or all of the default risk—a subsidy conveyed by lower interest payments. Also, the federal government either levies no loan guarantee fee or charges a smaller fee than a private insurer would charge. Consequently, a private lender with a federal guarantee can charge the borrower a lower interest rate. In addition, with some

guaranteed loans the federal government may pay to the lender part of the interest due on a guaranteed loan.[11]

Thus, a federal loan guarantee with or without a federal interest payment may provide a lower, equal, or higher level of subsidy than a federal direct loan.

## Concept of the Unified Budget

An important budget reform that preceded credit reform was the adoption of a unified budget. Before 1967, the federal government most frequently used an administrative budget, which was not comprehensive in coverage because it excluded the trust funds (for example, the Social Security trust fund). The federal government also used two other broad budgets: the consolidated cash budget and the national income accounts budget. Each of these three budgets had a different coverage of federal programs and a different accounting method; consequently each had a different surplus or deficit.[12] Each of these budgets had weaknesses, and the simultaneous use of three different budget concepts caused confusion.[13] An important budget reform that preceded credit reform was the adoption of a unified budget.

In March 1967, the President's Commission on Budget Concepts was created and instructed to make "a thorough and objective review of budgetary concepts."[14] In October 1967, the commission produced a comprehensive report with detailed recommendations on implementing a unified budget. In its report, the commission stated that the two basic functions of the federal budget are resource allocation and macroeconomic stabilization.[15] For resource allocation, the commission believed that the budget should "provide the integrated framework for information and analyses from which the best possible choices can be made in allocating the public's money among competing claims."[16] This function of resource allocation should include comparisons among government programs and between the public and private sectors.[17] For macroeconomic stabilization, the commission maintained that the budget should contain detailed and accurate information in order to evaluate the effects of federal fiscal activities.

Furthermore, the commission stated that the budget should include data necessary to undertake discretionary countercyclical fiscal policy.[18] Thus, the commission recommended a unified budget that would be composed of all federal activities, including the trust funds and federal credit activities. The commission recommended that federal credit programs be measured by their cash flows, although it realized that this procedure provided a poor measure of the economic and budgetary effects of federal credit. In the FY1969 budget, the Johnson Administration adopted the unified budget concept, but with some structural differences from the proposal of the commission. The Johnson Administration essentially adopted commission recommendations of measuring credit by its cash flows.

Subsequent implementation of federal credit reform would improve the use of the unified budget for resource allocation and macroeconomic stabilization as originally desired by the commission.[19]

# FEDERAL CREDIT REFORM ACT OF 1990

Some budget experts and policymakers criticized the cash flow treatment of federal credit in the unified budget as not accurately measuring the cost of federal credit and its effect on resource allocation. Beginning in 1983, proposals for using accrual accounting for federal credit were debated and culminated in the Federal Credit Reform Act of 1990, which is the basis for the treatment of federal credit today.[20]

The four stated purposes of the FCRA were listed in Section 501:

(1) measure more accurately the costs of federal credit programs;
(2) place the cost of credit programs on a budgetary basis equivalent to other federal spending;
(3) encourage the delivery of benefits in the form most appropriate to the needs of beneficiaries; and
(4) improve the allocation of resources among credit programs and other spending.

## Subsidy Costs

The FCRA never uses the word subsidy; nevertheless, the budgetary and economic cost of a federal credit program is arguably the subsidy value at the time credit is provided. The FCRA defines [subsidy] cost as "the estimated long-term cost to the government of a direct loan or loan guarantee, calculated on net present value basis, excluding administrative costs and any incidental effects on governmental receipts or outlays" [Section 502(5A)]. The discount rate used to calculate subsidy costs in terms of present value is the "average interest rate on marketable Treasury securities of similar maturity" [Section 502(5E)].[21] Hence, the subsidy cost of a program is determined by the amount of credit provided and the discount rate used to calculate the net present value of that credit.

Any government action that changes the estimated present value of an outstanding federal credit program is counted in the budget in the year in which the change occurs as a change in the subsidy cost of that program [Section 502(5D)]. For example, the federal government could partially forgive the repayment of principal for low-income borrowers from a particular credit program, which would increase the subsidy cost of the program.

## Estimation of Subsidies

The director of the Office of Management and Budget is responsible for coordinating the estimation of subsidy costs. "The Director may delegate to agencies authority to make estimates of costs" [Section 503(a)]. But agencies must use written guidelines from the director, which are developed after consultation with the director of the Congressional Budget Office. The director of OMB and the director of CBO are responsible for developing more accurate historical data on credit programs, which are used to estimate subsidy costs (Section 503). The President's budget includes "the planned level of new direct loan obligations and new loan guarantee commitments associated with each appropriations request" (Section 504).

## Budgetary Treatment

Beginning with FY1992, an appropriation for the annual subsidy cost of each credit program is made into a budget account called a *credit program account*. The subsidy cost of federal credit is scored as an outlay in the fiscal year in which the credit is disbursed by either the federal government or a private lender [Section 504(d)].

Discretionary programs providing new direct loan obligations and new loan guarantee commitments require appropriations of budget authority equal to their estimated subsidy costs. Funding for the subsidy costs of discretionary credit programs is provided in appropriation acts and must compete with other discretionary programs for funding available under the constraints of a budget resolution.

Mandatory programs, generally credit entitlements (for example, guaranteed student loans), and existing credit programs of the Commodity Credit Corporation have indefinite budget authority [Section 505(a-c)]. Most mandatory credit programs receive automatic funding for the amount of credit needed to meet the estimated demand by beneficiaries, which depends on eligibility and benefits rules contained in substantive law. For mandatory credit programs, any additional cost from reestimates of subsidies for a credit program is covered by permanent indefinite budget authority. This additional cost is displayed in a subaccount in the credit program account.

Also, beginning with FY1992, each credit program has a nonbudget financing account. Each of these nonbudget financing accounts receives payments from its associated credit program account equal to the subsidy cost at the time a new loan or loan guarantee is provided.

The financing account for each new direct loan also acquires the value of the unsubsidized portion of that loan (actual disbursements by the government minus the subsidy cost). This amount is borrowed from the Treasury through the loan program.[22]

Furthermore, the financing accounts contain all other cash flows between the public and the government associated with each credit program [Section 502(5E6-7)]. These flows include "the disbursement and repayment of loans, the payment of default losses on guarantees, and the collection of interest and fees."[23] Because they are nonbudget, the cash flows into and out of these accounts are not reflected in total outlay, receipts, or surplus/deficit. The budget authority of a credit program provides the means for the credit program account to pay to the financing account an amount equal to that program's estimated subsidy costs. The off-budget borrowing from the Treasury for the unsubsidized portion of a direct loan program is included in the national debt.

Another special account, the *liquidating account*, includes all ongoing cash flows of each credit program resulting from credit advanced prior to October 1, 1991 [Section 502(5E8)]. However, the budgetary procedures under the FCRA would apply to modifications made by the U.S. government to credit terms on credit provided before FY1992.[24]

The FCRA does not apply to the credit activities of the Federal Deposit Insurance Corporation, the National Credit Union Administration, the Resolution Trust Corporation, national flood insurance, the National Insurance Development Fund, crop insurance, or the Tennessee Valley Authority (Section 506).

# IMPLEMENTATION

## Federal Agencies

The Federal Credit Reform Act of 1990 was brief as a policy statement; it covered only five and one-half pages of the *U.S. Code, Congressional and Administrative News*.[25] Numerous details necessary to make the act operational were absent. Furthermore, many federal agencies had inadequate financial and accounting systems to implement credit reform.[26]

On July 2, 1992, OMB issued a revised circular, which improved and clarified instructions for credit budget formulation.[27] Furthermore, OMB simplified its credit subsidy model to help agencies to estimate direct loan and loan guarantee subsidies.[28] In November 2000, OMB updated Circular A-129 concerning the budgetary treatment of federal credit programs.[29] On November 2, 2005, OMB also revised Circular A-11 to include federal credit reform procedures. In Circular A-11, OMB explains how agencies should fill out credit schedules in preparing their budget requests.[30] Federal agencies working with OMB have steadily improved their compliance with credit reform standards.

Since the passage of the FCRA, OMB has continued to assist agencies in upgrading the quality of subsidy estimates. Beginning with FY1994, agencies have recorded reestimates of the cost of their credit programs, and aggregate subsidy estimates have been adjusted upward or downward annually.[31] The FCRA provided for permanent indefinite authority to cover the cost of reestimates so that new appropriations would not be needed. Agencies are required to incorporate improved knowledge into their subsidy estimates for future direct loan obligations and loan guarantee commitments.[32]

The Government Accountability Office examined subsidy estimates for 10 credit programs in five agencies for the period of fiscal years 1992 through 1998. GAO found problems with supporting documentation for subsidy estimates and the reliability of subsidy rate estimates and reestimates in each agency.[33] But GAO concluded that agencies showed improvement in documenting their estimates.[34]

CBO examined credit subsidy re-estimates for the period of FY1993 through FY1999. CBO concluded that

> Projecting the losses and costs from federal credit assistance is difficult, and errors are inevitable. Although various incentives may exist for agencies to underestimate credit subsidies, the Congressional Budget

> Office's analysis of corrected reestimates does not reveal any pattern of bias in initial subsidy estimates. However, another problem was uncovered: the reestimates reported in the president's budget are in such disorder that analysts cannot rely on them. A few modest changes in current practice could reduce agencies' errors in preparing, reporting, and accounting for estimates and reestimates.[35]

OMB established on-budget *receipt accounts* to receive payments of earnings from the financing accounts in those cases where federal credit programs are estimated to produce net income, that is, have negative subsidies.[36] Usually, payments into a program's receipt account are recorded in the Treasury's general fund as offsetting receipts.[37] "In a few cases, the receipts are earmarked in a special fund established for the program and are available for appropriation for the program."[38]

## Federal Accounting Standards Advisory Board

In October 1990, the Federal Accounting Standards Advisory Board (FASAB or "the Board") was established by the Secretary of the Treasury, the director of OMB, and the Comptroller General to consider and recommend accounting principles for the federal government. On September 15, 1992, the board issued an exposure draft recommending accounting standards for federal credit programs on a basis consistent with credit reform. The board received numerous substantive comments that were considered in revising its exposure draft, and on August 23, 1993, OMB issued the board's revised report titled *Accounting for Direct Loans and Loan Guarantees*.[39] This report provided extensive detail, including numerous arithmetic examples, clarifying credit reform practices.[40] It further required that federal agencies use of present value accounting for federal credit programs be consistent with the Federal Credit Reform Act of 1990.[41] Thus, for their credit programs, agencies' accounting procedures were now required to be consistent with their budgetary procedures.

## Balanced Budget Act of 1997

On August 5, 1997, the Balanced Budget Act of 1997 was enacted. This law amended the Federal Credit Reform Act of 1990 to make some technical changes including codifying several OMB guidelines. The law made important changes that continue to govern federal credit today:

First, agencies are required to use the same discount rate to calculate the subsidy when they obligate budget authority for direct loans and loan guarantees and when submitting the agency's budget justification for the President's budget.[42] Thus, the dollar value of loans for a specific credit program is known when Congress considers subsidy appropriations for that program. Prior to this change, agencies had used interest rates from the preceding calendar quarter to calculate the subsidy at the time a direct loan was advanced or a loan guarantee was obligated.[43]

Second, agencies are required to use the same forecast assumptions (for example, default and recovery rates) to calculate subsidy rates when they obligate credit and when preparing the President's budget.[44]

Third, agencies are required to transfer end-of-year unobligated balances in liquidating accounts (revolving funds for direct loans and loan guarantees made prior to the effective date of the FCRA) to the general fund as soon as practicable after the close of the fiscal year.[45]

Fourth, the same interest rate must be used on financing account debt (which generates interest payments to the Treasury), financing account balances, and the discount rate used to calculate subsidy costs.[46]

Fifth, the definition of the term "cost" was modified so that the discount rate is based on the timing of cash flows instead of on the term of the loan. Under this new approach, in the President's budget, a series of different rates would be used to calculate the present value of cost flows over a multi-year period. For example, for a 10-year direct loan (or loan guarantee), costs in the first year would be discounted using the interest rate on a one-year Treasury bill, costs in the second year would be discounted using the interest rate on a two-year Treasury note, etc. Under the prior approach, the interest rate of a 10-year Treasury note would have been used as the discount rate. The earlier method proved to be inferior because the flow of semiannual interest payments and the repayment of full principal on the last payment date did not match up well with yearly cost flows.[47]

## Possible Payment of Subsidy Costs by Recipients

Rather than having the federal government pay for the subsidy costs of credit programs, a credit program may result in some cases in the subsidy costs being paid by credit recipients. For example, the Energy Policy Act of 2005

(P.L. 109-58; 119 Stat. 594) includes Title XVII— Incentives for Innovative Technologies. Section 1702 (b) states that

> No [loan] guarantee shall be made unless—(1) an appropriation for the cost has been made; or (2) the Secretary [of Energy] has received from the borrower a payment in full for the cost of the obligation and deposited the payment into the Treasury.

If credit recipients pay the subsidy costs and there is no ceiling on appropriations, then hypothetically there would be no limit to the size of the loan guarantee program. But this law does not state anything about an appropriations ceiling on the volume of loan guarantees. Some observers argue that loan guarantees with the recipients paying the estimated costs should not be provided unless there is a cap on appropriations in order to control the size of a credit program.[48] No loan guarantees for innovative fuel technology have been made in which the credit recipient has paid the estimated subsidy cost upfront.

## Federal Credit in the President's FY2013 Budget

In the Federal Credit Supplement for the FY2013 budget, OMB presents the loan characteristic variables for each credit program, which are loan maturity period, borrower interest rate, grace period, upfront fees, annual fees, other fees, assumed default rate, rate of recovery on defaults, and percent of loan guaranteed (for loan guarantee programs only).[49] In addition, OMB breaks down estimated subsidy rates into four components: defaults (net of recoveries), interest, fees, and all other.[50]

For FY2013, OMB estimates an aggregate proposed subsidy budget authority of *new direct loans* of negative $33.352 billion.[51] This high negative subsidy budget authority amount was due, almost exclusively, to negative proposed subsidy budget authority of new direct loans for the Department of Education's Federal Direct Student Loan Program (negative $33.475 billion).[52] This high negative subsidy level was due primarily to the use of Treasury interest rates to discount future credit flows. Fair value budgeting, an alternative method of discounting future credit flows, is discussed in the next section.

For FY2013, OMB estimates an aggregate proposed subsidy budget authority of *new loan guarantees* of negative $9.467 billion.[53] This high negative subsidy budget authority amount was due primarily to negative proposed subsidy budget authority of new loan guarantees for the FHA-Mutual Mortgage Insurance Program Account[54] of negative $8.188 billion.[55]

# Proposals for the Expansion of Reforms

Four major proposals to expand credit reform have been discussed in recent years. Some of these proposed expansions are also included in legislation described in the next section on proposed legislation in the 112th Congress.

## Inclusion of Government-Sponsored Enterprises

The principles of credit reform could be applied to government-sponsored enterprises (GSEs). GSEs are privately owned financial intermediaries, which were established and chartered by the federal government. GSEs pay lower interest rates on their securities because investors generally believe that securities issued by GSEs have an implied federal guarantee, making them appear less risky than other private sector securities.

Proponents of extending credit reform principles to GSEs have argued that the federal government has already "bailed out" one GSE (the Farm Credit System). In the late 1970s, agricultural prices declined, farm income plummeted, and agricultural land prices fell.[56] Consequently, many farmers were unable to repay their loans and the Farm Credit System incurred large losses. A series of federal efforts to assist the Farm Credit System were unsuccessful, and eventually lead to the enactment of the Agriculture Credit Act of 1987 (P.L. 100-233) on January 6, 1988.[57] This act provided federal financial assistance to prevent the Farm Credit System from defaulting on its debt. Two decades later, on September 7, 2008, the federal government placed in conservatorship or receivership two financially troubled housing GSEs: the Federal National Mortgage Association (Fannie Mae) and the Federal Home Loan Mortgage Corporation (Freddie Mac).[58] Legislation has been proposed to reform these housing enterprises.[59] Hence, proponents argue that credit reform should cover the subsidy costs to taxpayers of all GSEs.

Opponents have argued that the subsidy costs of GSEs are difficult to quantify; furthermore, the federal government has no legal responsibility to "bail out" GSEs. Opponents also maintain that the current low Treasury interest rates and the exclusion of both administrative costs and risk premiums may result in negative subsidy costs for GSEs.

## Extension to Federal Insurance

The principles of credit reform could be extended to federal insurance, which is treated primarily on a cash flow basis.[60] Most federal insurance consists of deposit insurance or pension insurance.[61]

The Government Accountability Office maintains that credit reform could improve the budgetary information and incentives for federal insurance.[62] But, for some federal insurance programs, significant difficulties exist in accurately estimating future claims for losses. Often, historical data are unavailable, frequent program modifications occur, and fundamental changes take place in the activities insured.[63]

Many federal insurance programs cover types of risk that the private sector has either refused or been unable to cover.[64]

> The complexity of the issues involved and the need to build agency capacity to generate such estimates suggest that it is not feasible to integrate accrual-based costs directly into the budget at this time.[65]

GAO has suggested that a supplemental approach should precede the full inclusion of insurance programs under credit reform. Thus, GAO has recommended that accrual-based cost measures be initially included along with cash-based estimates as supplemental information in the budget documents.[66]

On April 25, 2002, GAO's director of federal budget analysis gave the following testimony before the House Committee on the budget:

> While there are significant estimation and implementation challenges, accrual-based budgeting has the potential to improve budgetary information and incentives for these programs by providing more accurate and timely recognition of the government's costs and improving the information and incentives for managing insurance costs.
>
> In 1997 we reported that the current cash-based budget generally provides incomplete information on the costs of federal insurance programs. The ultimate costs to the federal government may not be apparent up front because of time lags between the extension of the insurance, the receipt of premiums, and the payment of claims.[67]

Some opponents of the inclusion of insurance programs maintain that, because the current subsidy measure excludes administrative costs and a risk premium, some major insurance programs would record negative subsidies.

## Inclusion of Market Risk

The budgetary cost to taxpayers of providing federal credit could be changed to include market risk.[68] When credit reform was debated, the Government Accountability Office (GAO), the Congressional Budget Office (CBO), the Office of Management and Budget (OMB), and the Senate Budget Committee all recommended that federal credit be measured by the net present value of credit subsidies.[69] But, GAO and the Senate Budget Committee recommended a cost-to-the-government measure be used while CBO and OMB supported a "market-valuation oriented measurement approach, which calculates the economic benefit borrowers receive as a result of obtaining federal, rather than private sector, loans."[70]

Currently, the FCRA requires the discounting of expected cash flows at the interest rate on Treasury securities (the rate at which the government borrows money). CBO's report on federal credit subsidies examined two ways of including the market price for risk: risk-adjusted discount rates and options-pricing methods.

The risk-adjusted discount rate (ADR) method "adds a spread—the difference between the interest rate on a Treasury security and the rate on a risky security—to Treasury rates and uses the resulting adjusted rate to discount expected cash flows associated with a loan."[71] The ADR method results in a higher discount rate for both costs and revenues and, with a few exceptions for negative subsidies, raises the net cost of credit programs.

An option is a contract that gives the buyer the right, but not the obligation, to buy or sell a specified quantity of an instrument at a specific price within a specified period of time, regardless of the market price of that instrument.[72] "The general idea behind options-pricing methods is that assets with the same payoffs must have the same price; otherwise, investors would have the opportunity to earn a risk-free profit by buying low and selling high."[73] An options-pricing method is likely to be more accurate than the ADR method but only when the necessary data and model are available.[74] Options-pricing models are seldom used to value credit provided to individuals; instead the use of the ADR method is usually appropriate.[75] Option-pricing methods are usually better than ADR methods in valuing credit provided to commercial enterprises.[76] The best method to use varies for other credit programs such as "loan assistance to sovereign states, municipalities, and special-purpose enterprises."[77]

As an example of the process, CBO applied a type of options pricing—the binomial pricing method—to calculate the risk-adjusted cost of extending federal loan guarantees to Chrysler in 1980 and to America West Airlines (AWA) in 2002. CBO computed that the market-value loss of the Chrysler loan guarantee was $239.0 million instead of the Treasury-rate loss of $107.6 million.[78] CBO also found that the calculated market-value loss was $26.3 million for the AWA loan guarantee instead of a gain of $47.4 million using Treasury interest rates.[79]

In the President's budget for FY2013, the Office of Management and Budget selected "Fair Value Budgeting for Credit Programs" as a topic for in-depth analysis.[80] OMB compared and contrasted the current cost to the government with fair value budgeting. In March 2012, CBO released an issue brief titled *Fair-Value Accounting for Federal Credit Programs*.[81] CBO indicated its support for fair value accounting, but acknowledged that fair value accounting involves implementation issues.

CBO stated that "the government already uses fair-value estimates in budgeting for a few types of programs or transactions, including commitments of resources for some International Monetary Fund lending facilities and the Troubled Asset Relief Program."[82]

The weak economy and expansionary monetary policy caused low nominal Treasury interest rates from FY2009-FY2011. Consequently, the use of Treasury interest rates in the cost to the government measure resulted in aggregate costs of federal credit of negative $19 billion for FY2009, negative $20 billion for FY2010, and negative $41 billion for FY2011.[83] These negative costs reduced the sizes of the federal deficits. In contrast, the aggregate cost of federal credit averaged positive $3.1 billion annually for FY1998-FY2008.[84] Arguably, these negative aggregate costs of federal credit over the past three fiscal years have contributed to the debate about changing to fair value budgeting.[85]

## Inclusion of Administrative Costs

As was discussed in the 1990 debate, administrative costs of credit programs could be included in the calculation of the costs of these programs. Proponents argue that the current exclusion of these costs understates the actual costs of credit programs. Proponents also stress that cost comparisons among credit programs are distorted. For example, the administrative costs per $1 million of credit are higher for direct student loans than guaranteed student loans. Opponents argue that agencies have difficulty separating the administrative costs of their credit programs from their general administrative costs.

In its analysis of fair-value budgeting, CBO stated,

> Comprehensive fair-value estimates of subsidies for credit programs would incorporate certain administrative expenses, such as servicing and collection costs, that are essential to preserving the value of the government's claims (rather than accounting separately for those costs on a cash basis). Those essential preservation expenses can differ significantly among credit programs, and including them in subsidy cost estimates would make comparing various subsidy costs easier. However, doing so could erode Congressional control over program expenditures because, under FCRA, all increases in estimated costs after a loan or loan guarantee is initiated (including those arising from increased expenditures on servicing or loan collection) are automatically appropriated. Another concern is that implementing a switch from cash to accrual accounting for essential preservation expenses would be administratively complicated.[86]

# PROPOSED LEGISLATION IN THE 112TH CONGRESS

Four bills have been introduced in the 112th Congress that include major proposals to reform the budgetary treatment of federal credit. Some of the reforms in these proposals were discussed extensively in the prior section of this report.[87]

## S. 1651/H.R. 3414. Honest Budget Act

S. 1651 and H.R. 3414 are related bills. On October 4, 2011, Senator Jeff Sessions introduced S. 1651. On November 14, 2011, Representative Bill Huizenga introduced H.R. 3414.

The first purpose of these bills is identified as "to measure more accurately the costs of Federal credit programs by accounting for them on a fair value basis."[88] These bills define the term "cost" as "the sum of the Treasury discounting component and the risk component of a direct loan, loan guarantee, or financial investment or a modification thereof."[89] Beginning with FY2015, these bills expand the coverage of FCRA to include "financial investment programs."[90] These bills define the term financial investment as "an investment by the Government in any securities (debt or equity), stock, bonds, or futures, options, swaps, or other derivatives, issued by a non-federal entity...."[91] These bills state that "all funding for an agency's administrative costs associated with a direct loan, loan guarantee, or financial investment program shall be displayed as distinct and separately identified subaccounts within the same budget account as the program's cost."[92]

## H.R. 3581. Budget and Accounting Transparency Act of 2011

On December 7, 2011, Representative Scott Garrett introduced H.R. 3581. On February 7, 2012, the bill passed the House by a 245-180 vote.[93] On February 9, this act was referred to the Senate Committee on the Budget.

The first purpose identified in this bill is "to measure more accurately the costs of Federal Credit programs by accounting for them on a fair value basis."[94] This bill defines the term "cost" as "the sum of the Treasury discounting component and the risk component of a direct loan, loan guarantee, or financial investment or a modification thereof."[95] This bill states that

> Not later than 1 year after the date of enactment of this Act, the Directors of the Congressional Budget Office and the Office of Management and Budget shall each prepare a study and make recommendations to the Committees on the Budget of the House of Representatives and the Senate as to the feasibility of applying fair value concepts to budgeting for the costs of Federal insurance programs.[96]

This bill would require that the receipts and disbursements of the Federal National Mortgage Association (Fannie Mae) and the Federal Home Loan Mortgage Corporation (Freddie Mac) be included in the budget.[97] FCRA would thereby apply to these GSEs.

## H.R. 3844. Honest Budget Act of 2012

On January 31, 2012, Representative Martha Roby introduced H.R. 3844. The sections concerning the budgetary treatment of federal credit are essentially the same as in the Honest Budget Act (S. 1651/H.R. 3414), which was described above.

# APPENDIX A. CONCEPTS OF PRESENT VALUE AND FUTURE VALUE

The concepts of present value and future value can be explained by using simple examples.[98] A dollar received now is more valuable than a dollar received a year from now for the simple reason that if you have a dollar today, you can put it in the bank and have more than a dollar a year from now because of interest earning. Since dollars today are worth more than dollars in the future, we need some means of weighting cash flows that are received at different times in order that they can be compared. Mathematics provides us with the means of making such comparisons. With a few simple calculations, we can adjust the value of a dollar received any number of years from now in order that it can be compared with the value of a dollar in hand today.

**The Mathematics of Interest:**

The future value of an investment can be expressed in mathematical terms by means of the following formula or equation:

$$\mathbf{Fn = P(1 + r)^n}$$

where: Fn = the balance (or future value) at the end of period n, P = the amount invested now, r = the rate of interest per period, and the n exponent is the number of periods.

**Examples:**

(1) Assume \$100 is deposited in a bank saving account for one year, at an interest rate of 5%. Then P = \$100, r = 0.05, and n = 1. Under these conditions, the future value at the end of year 1 or F1 = \$105.
The \$100 present outlay is called the present value of the \$105 amount to be received in one year. It is also known as the discounted value of the future \$105 receipt.

(2) Assume that the \$105 is left in the bank for a second year at an interest rate of 5%. Thus, the initial \$100 compounds over a two year period. Then P = \$100, r = 0.05, and n = 2. Under these conditions, the future value at the end of year 2 or F2 = \$110.25. Thus, at the end of the second year the original \$100 deposit will have grown to \$110.25.

The \$100 present outlay is called the present value of the \$110.25 amount to be received in two years. It is also know as the discounted value of the future \$110.25 receipt.

The **present value** of any sum to be received in the future can be computed by turning the equation for future value or $\mathbf{Fn = P(1 + r)^{n}}$ around and solving for P: $\mathbf{P = Fn/(1 + r)^{n}}$.

## APPENDIX B. FEDERAL CREDIT DATA

**Table B-1. Estimated Future Cost of Outstanding Federal Credit Programs, FY2011 (in billions of dollars)**

| Program | Outstanding 2011 | Estimated Future Costs of 2011 Outstanding[a] |
|---|---|---|
| **Direct Loans:**[b] | | |
| Federal Student Loans | 378 | –14 |
| GSE Mortgage-Backed Securities Purchase Program | 71 | –2 |
| Troubled Asset Relief Program[c] | 100 | 42 |
| Education Temporary Student Loan Purchase Authority | 98 | –13 |
| Farm Service Agency (excl. CCC), Rural Development, Rural Housing | 52 | 10 |
| Rural Utilities Service and Rural Telephone Bank | 47 | 2 |
| State Housing Finance Authority Direct Loans | 15 | 1 |
| Disaster Assistance | 8 | 2 |
| Housing and Urban Development | 9 | 7 |
| Export-Import Bank | 9 | 2 |
| Public Law 480 | 5 | 2 |
| Agency for International Development | 4 | 1 |
| Department of Energy, Title 17, ATVM | 7 | 1 |
| Small Business Lending Fund[c] | 4 | –* |

| Program | Outstanding 2011 | Estimated Future Costs of 2011 Outstanding[a] |
|---|---|---|
| Other direct loan programs[c] | 31 | 11 |
| Total direct loans | 838 | 52 |
| **Guaranteed Loans:**[b] | | |
| FHA-Mutual Mortgage Insurance Fund | 1,043 | 28 |
| Federal Student Loans | 328 | 10 |
| Department of Veterans Affairs (VA) Mortgages | 258 | 5 |
| FHA-General and Special Risk Insurance Fund | 138 | 8 |
| Small Business Administration (SBA)[d] | 82 | 5 |
| Farm Service Agency (excl. CCC), Rural Development, Rural Housing | 83 | 4 |
| Export-Import Bank | 49 | 1 |
| International Assistance | 20 | 3 |
| Commodity Credit Corporation | 6 | * |
| Government National Mortgage Association (GNMA) | ……… | * |
| Other guaranteed loan programs[e] | 10 | 1 |
| Total guaranteed loans | 2,017 | 64 |
| **Total Federal Credit** | **2,855** | **116** |

Source: Adapted by CRS from U.S. Executive Office of the President. Office of Management and Budget. *Analytical Perspectives, Budget of the United States Government, Fiscal Year 2013* (Washington: GPO, 2012), p. 401.

Notes: * = $500 million or less.

a. Direct loan future costs reflect the financing account allowance for subsidy cost and the liquidating account allowance for estimated uncollectible principal and interest. Loan guarantee future costs reflect estimated liabilities for loan guarantees

b. Excludes loans and guarantees by deposit insurance agencies and programs not included under credit reform, such as Commodity Credit Corporation (CCC) commodity price supports. Defaulted guaranteed loans that result in loans receivable are included in direct loan amounts.

c. As authorized by law, equity purchases under the TARP, the Small Business Lending Fund, and IMF Quota transactions provided in the Supplemental Appropriations Act of 2009 are included in the table. Future costs for TARP and IMF transactions reflected here are calculated using the discount rate required by the FCRA, adjusted for market risks, as directed in legislation.

d. Certain SBA data are excluded from the totals because they are secondary guarantees on SBA's own guaranteed loans. GNMA guarantee data are excluded from the totals because they are secondary guarantees on loans guaranteed by FHA, VA and RHS.

e. Includes Department of Energy Title 17 loan guarantees financed by private lenders.

# Appendix C. Budgetary Treatment of Federal Credit before FY1992

Before the implementation of the Federal Credit Reform Act of 1990, the unified budget treated federal credit in two different ways. The unified budget measured credit by its cash flows, but also, after 1980, included a separate credit budget that measured and selectively controlled gross credit flows.

## Unified Budget

The federal unified budget used cash-basis accounting. Before FY1992, a new federal direct loan was treated as a budget outlay in the current fiscal year, and repayments of principal and payments of interest were treated as offsetting collections (negative outlays) in the future fiscal years in which they occurred. If a loan recipient paid a fee, this fee was treated as an offsetting collection. Loan defaults reduced repayments of principal and interest, and therefore offsetting collections. Administrative expenses were reported as outlays. In a given fiscal year, the budgetary cost of a loan program, not the individual loans, was its net cash flow. This equaled new loans made plus any administrative expenses associated with these loans (rarely recognized in the loan accounts) less any loan fees, repayments of principal, and payments of interest.

The federal acceptance of a contingent liability when a loan guarantee was provided was not included in the federal budget because no cash flow occurred. The administrative costs of a guarantee program were outlays in the fiscal year in which they occurred. Some guarantee programs charge fees to the recipient, and these fees were considered offsetting collections. Any federal outlays necessary to compensate lenders for any default losses covered by a federal guarantee were not shown in the budget until they were actually paid.

## Credit Budget

In January 1980, the Office of Management and Budget introduced a federal "credit budget" to help monitor and control the growth of federal credit, including new direct loan obligations and new loan guarantee commitments. Federal credit was measured at the time that the government signed a binding contract to provide credit assistance. Initially, the credit budget consisted of nonbinding targets. Before FY1992, limits in the credit budget were included in the budget resolution and in annual appropriation acts for discretionary credit programs but not mandatory credit programs.[99] Although the credit budget improved credit visibility, the credit budget did not measure or control the size of subsidies.

The Federal Credit Reform Act of 1990 decreased the importance of the credit budget because control of credit subsidies largely replaced limits on gross credit flows as a determinant of the amount of new federal credit for each program. Estimated limitations on credit loan levels are proposed in each presidential budget, although the term "credit budget" is not used by OMB.[100] But these limitations on credit loan levels are set too high to realistically affect the amount of credit extended.

## Appendix D. Budgetary Treatment of a Hypothetical Direct Loan

(1) For a proposed direct loan program, CBO is required to estimate the subsidy cost if a bill including the loan program goes to the floor. If legislation is passed that includes a new loan program, OMB becomes responsible for estimating the subsidy cost. If a direct loan program "L" has been enacted into law, agency "A" establishes a credit program account and a nonbudget financing account.

(2) OMB in consultation with agency A estimates that the net present value of the cost of credit subsidies equals (in this example) 20% of loans disbursed under program L operated by agency A.

(3) If program L is a discretionary loan program, an appropriations bill for the fiscal year is passed by Congress and signed into law by the President.[101] This bill includes an appropriation of (in this example) $100 million for the subsidy budget authority of program L. Within agency A, this $100 million is appropriated to the credit program account for program L. Furthermore, this appropriations bill must include an estimate of the dollar amount of new direct loan obligations supportable by the subsidy budget authority appropriated to agency A for program L. For example, if program L has an

estimated subsidy rate of 20%, the dollar amount of new direct loan obligations supportable would be $500 million.

(4) Agency A signs a contract to loan $10 million to a borrower under the auspices of program L. The estimated subsidy cost of this loan is $2 million (20% of $10 million).

(5) The borrower meets the terms and conditions of the loan contract. Agency A pays $2 million from its credit program account for L into its financing account for L. The financing account for program L borrows $8 million (unsubsidized portion of the loan) from the U.S. Treasury. At the same time that these budgetary transfers occur within agency A, the loan of $10 million is disbursed from the financing account for program L to the borrower. The subsidy payment of $2 million that goes into the financing account is scored as an outlay for agency A and for the federal budget. The $8 million borrowed from the Treasury is a non-budget means of financing, and consequently, does not affect the budget deficit, outlays, or revenues. But this $8 million, if the budget is in deficit, does increase the national debt.

(6) Agency A services the loan. Cash flows between the public and the non-budget financing account for fees, interest, defaults, etc., do not affect the budget deficit, outlays, or revenues. But the net cash flows of the financing account do affect the national debt.

(7) Repayments of principal and payments of interest are paid by the borrower into the financing account for program L. The financing account uses these monies to pay the interest and repay the principal on the $8 million borrowed from the Treasury.

## APPENDIX E. BUDGETARY TREATMENT OF A HYPOTHETICAL LOAN GUARANTEE

(1) For a proposed loan guarantee program, CBO would be required to estimate the subsidy cost if a bill including the loan guarantee program goes to the floor. If legislation is passed that includes a new loan guarantee program, OMB becomes responsible for estimating the subsidy cost. If a loan guarantee program “G” has been enacted into law, agency “A” establishes a credit program account and a financing account.

(2) OMB in consultation with agency A estimates that the net present value of the cost of credit subsidies equals (in this example) 10% of loans guaranteed under program G operated by agency A.
(3) If program G is a discretionary loan guarantee program, an appropriations bill for the fiscal year is passed by Congress and signed into law by the President.[102] This bill includes an appropriation (in this example) of $60 million for the subsidy budget authority for program G. Within agency A, this $60 million is placed in the credit program account for program G. Furthermore, this appropriations bill must include an estimate of the dollar amount of guaranteed loan commitments supportable by the subsidy budget authority appropriated to agency A for program G. For example, if program G has an estimated subsidy rate of 10%, the dollar amount of new guaranteed loan commitments supportable would be $600 million.
(4) Agency A signs a contract to guarantee a loan of $15 million to the borrower. The estimated subsidy cost of this guarantee is $1.5 million (10% of $15 million). The loan guarantee fee (if any) is paid by the borrower to the financing account for program G at the time the loan guarantee is obligated.
(5) After the borrower (lender, or other party to the agreement) meets the terms and conditions of the loan guarantee contract, the borrower obtains the loan from the lender in the private sector. Agency A pays $1.5 million from its credit program account for G into its financing account for G. At the same time that this budgetary transfer occurs within agency A, the agency provides the guarantee in order for the borrower to obtain the loan from the private lender. The subsidy payment of $1.5 million that goes into the financing account is scored as an outlay for agency A and for the federal budget. The borrower must pay to the lender interest on the principal and repay the principal.
(6) Agency A services the loan guarantee. The cash flows between the public and the non-budget financing account do not affect the budget deficit, outlays, or revenues. But the net cash flow from the financing account affects the national debt.
(7) The subsidy amount and any loan guarantee fee earn interest, which is paid by the Treasury. If the borrower defaults on all or part of the guaranteed loan then the financing account is responsible for covering the cost of compensating the lender.

# Appendix F. Direct Loan Data, FY2013

## Table F-1. Subsidy Rates, Budget Authority, and Loan Levels for Proposed Direct Loans for FY2013 (in millions of dollars and percent)

| Agency and Program | Subsidy Rate % | Subsidy Budget Authority $ | Loan Levels $ |
|---|---|---|---|
| **Agriculture:** | | | |
| Agricultural Credit Insurance Fund Program Account | 4.80 | 77 | 1,632 |
| Farm Storage Facility Loans Program Account | –2.47 | –7 | 303 |
| Rural Electrification and Telecommunications Loans Program Account | –5.55 | –377 | 6,790 |
| Distance Learning, Telemedicine, and Broadband Program | 9.47 | 9 | 94 |
| Rural Water and Waste Disposal Program Account | 8.07 | 90 | 1,121 |
| Rural Community Facilities Program Account | –2.08 | –42 | 2,000 |
| Farm Labor Program Account | ......... | ......... | ......... |
| Multifamily Housing Revitalization Program Account | 60.20 | 31 | 51 |
| Rural Housing Insurance Fund Program Account | 7.28 | 52 | 707 |
| Rural Microenterprise Investment Program Account | 14.95 | 5 | 34 |
| Rural Development Loan Fund Program Account | 32.04 | 6 | 19 |
| Rural Economic Development Loans Program Account | 12.39 | 4 | 33 |
| **Commerce:** | | | |
| Fisheries Finance Program Account | –4.21 | –4 | 83 |
| **Defense—Military:** | | | |
| Defense Family Housing Improvement Fund | ......... | ......... | ......... |
| **Education:** | | | |
| College Housing and Academic Facilities Loans | 6.29 | 20 | 320 |
| Teacher Education Assistance | 10.89 | 11 | 97 |
| Federal Perkins Loan Program Account | –29.10 | –1,379 | 4,737 |
| Federal Direct Student Loan Program Account | –20.08 | –33,475 | 166,707 |
| **Energy:** | | | |
| Title 17 Innovative Technology Loan Guarantee Program | .........[a] | ......... | 15,000 |
| Advanced Technology Vehicles Manufacturing Loan Program Account | ......... | ......... | ......... |
| **Health and Human Services:** | | | |
| Consumer Operated and Oriented Plan Program Account | 43.05 | 699 | 1,625 |
| **Homeland Security:** | | | |
| Disaster Assistance Direct Loan Program Account | –1.51 | –1 | 25 |
| **Housing and Urban Development:** | | | |
| FHA-Mutual Mortgage Insurance Program Account | ......... | ......... | 50 |
| FHA-General and Special Risk Program Account | ......... | ......... | 1 |
| Emergency Homeowners' Relief Fund | ......... | ......... | ......... |

| Agency and Program | Subsidy Rate % | Subsidy Budget Authority $ | Loan Levels $ |
|---|---|---|---|
| **State:** | | | |
| Repatriation Loans Program Account | 57.67 | 1 | 2 |
| **Transportation:** | | | |
| TIFIA General Fund Program Account, Federal Highway Administration, Transportation | 10.34 | 39 | 377 |
| Federal-aid Highways | 9.66 | 478 | 4,948 |
| Railroad Rehabilitation and Improvement Program | ......... | ......... | 600 |
| **Treasury:** | | | |
| Small Business Lending Fund Program Account[b] | ......... | ......... | ......... |
| Community Development Financial Institutions Fund Program Account | 0.78 | 8 | 1,025 |
| **Veterans Affairs:** | | | |
| Veterans Housing Benefit Program Fund | –2.54 | –33 | 1,326 |
| Native American Veteran Housing Loan | –13.87 | –2 | 14 |
| **International Assistance Programs:** | | | |
| Development Credit Authority Program Account | ......... | 34 | ......... |
| Overseas Private Investment Corporation | –3.10 | –36 | 1,150 |
| **Small Business Administration:** | | | |
| Disaster Loans Program Account | 11.11 | 122 | 1,100 |
| Business Loans Program Account | 15.71 | 3 | 18 |
| **Export-Import Bank of the United States:** | | | |
| Export-Import Bank loans Program Account | 30.08 | 8 | 25 |
| **National Infrastructure Bank:** | | | |
| National Infrastructure Bank Program Account | 15.02 | 338 | 2,250 |
| **Total** | **N/A** | **–33,352** | **214,274** |

Source: Adapted by CRS from U.S. Executive Office of the President. Office of Management and Budget, *Analytical Perspectives, Budget of the United States Government, Fiscal Year 2013* (Washington, DC: GPO, 2012), p. 405.

Notes: Additional information on credit subsidy rates is contained in the *Federal Credit Supplement* to the budget for 2013.

N/A = Not applicable.

a. Rate reflects notional estimate, including transactions funded through either appropriations or borrower fees. Estimates will be determined at the time of execution, and will reflect the terms of the contracts and other characteristics.

b. As authorized by law, equity purchases under the Small Business Lending Fund and IMF transactions provided in the Supplemental Appropriations Act of 2009 are included in the table.

# Appendix G. Loan Guarantee Data, FY2013

### Table G-1. Subsidy Rates, Budget Authority, and Loan Levels for Proposed Loan Guarantees for FY2013 (in millions of dollars and percent)

| Agency and Program | Subsidy Rate % | Subsidy Budget Authority $ | Loan Levels $ |
|---|---|---|---|
| **Agriculture:** | | | |
| Agriculture Credit Insurance Fund | 0.52 | 17 | 3,150 |
| Commodity Credit Corporation Export Loans | –0.81 | –45 | 5,500 |
| Rural Water and Waste Disposal Program Account | 1.06 | * | 47 |
| Rural Community Facilities Program Account | 6.75 | 1 | 16 |
| Rural Housing Insurance Fund Program Account | –0.28 | –67 | 24,150 |
| Rural Business Program Account | 6.86 | 67 | 981 |
| Rural Energy for America Program | 24.01 | 28 | 118 |
| **Commerce:** | | | |
| Economic Development Assistance Programs | 18.06 | 7 | 39 |
| **Energy:** | | | |
| Title 17 Innovative Technology Loan Guarantee Program | ......... | ......... | ......... |
| **Health and Human Services:** | | | |
| Health Resources and Services | 3.70 | * | 12 |
| **Housing and Urban Development:** | | | |
| Indian Housing Loan Guarantee Fund | 0.83 | 7 | 900 |
| Native Hawaiian Housing Loan Guarantee | 0.50 | 1 | 38 |
| Native American Housing Block Grant | 10.91 | 2 | 18 |
| Community Development Loan Guarantees | ......... | ......... | 500 |
| FHA-Mutual Mortgage Insurance | –3.73 | –8,188 | 219,562 |
| FHA-General and Special Risk | –4.01 | –661 | 16,435 |
| **Interior:** | | | |
| Indian Guaranteed Loan Program Account | 5.53 | 4 | 73 |
| **Transportation:** | | | |
| Minority Business Resource Center Program | 1.73 | * | 22 |
| Federal-Aid Highways | 9.50 | 20 | 211 |
| Railroad Rehabilitation and Improvement Program | ......... | ......... | 100 |
| Maritime Guaranteed Loan (Title XI) | ......... | ......... | ......... |
| **Veterans Affairs:** | | | |
| **Agriculture:** | | | |

| | | | |
|---|---|---|---|
| Veterans Housing Benefit Program Fund | 0.27 | 135 | 50,821 |
| **International Assistance Programs:** | | | |
| Loan Guarantees to Israel Program Account | ......... | ......... | ......... |
| Development Credit Authority Program Account | 6.45 | 47 | 729 |
| Overseas Private Investment Corporation | –6.38 | –185 | 2,900 |
| **Small Business Administration:** | | | |
| Disaster Loans Program Account | 2.31 | 1 | 57 |
| Business Loans Program Account | 0.45 | 374 | 83,440 |
| **Export-Import Bank of the United States:** | | | |
| Export-Import Bank Loans Program Account | –2.83 | –1,049 | 36,949 |
| **National Infrastructure Bank:** | | | |
| National Infrastructure Bank Program Account | 8.51 | 17 | 200 |
| **Total** | **N/A** | **–9,467** | **446,968** |
| **Addendum: Secondary Guaranteed Loan Commitments** | | | |
| **GNMA:** | | | |
| Guarantees of Mortgage-backed Securities Loan Guarantee Program Account | –0.23 | –550 | 239,000 |
| **Treasury:** | | | |
| Troubled Asset Relief Program, Housing Programs[a] | 4.76 | 2,466 | 51,862 |
| **SBA:** | | | |
| Secondary Market Guarantee Program | ......... | ......... | 12,000 |
| **Total, secondary guaranteed loan commitments** | **N/A** | **1,916** | **302,862** |

Source: Adapted by CRS from U.S. Executive Office of the President. Office of Management and Budget. *Analytical Perspectives, Budget of the United States Government, Fiscal Year 2013* (Washington, DC: GPO, 2012), p. 407.

Notes: Additional information on credit subsidy rates is contained in the Federal Credit Supplement.

N/A = Not applicable.

[*] = $500,000 or less.

[a]. Amounts reflect the TARP FHA Refinance Letter of Credit program. Subsidy costs for this program are calculated using the discount rate required by the FCRA, adjusted for market risks, as directed in legislation.

## End Notes

[1] Section 502(1) of the *Federal Credit Reform Act of 1990*.

[2] Section 502(3) of the *Federal Credit Reform Act of 1990*.

[3] U.S. Executive Office of the President, Office of Management and Budget, *Analytical Perspectives, Budget of the U.S. Government, Fiscal Year 2013* (Washington, DC: GPO, 2012), p. 401.

[4] The concepts of present value and future value are explained in examples in **Appendix A**.

[5] Some of these concepts and the budgetary treatment of federal credit before the FCRA are presented in more detail in the following source: James M. Bickley, "The Bush

Administration's Proposal for Credit Reform: Background, Analysis, and Policy Issues," *Public Budgeting & Finance*, vol. 11, no. 1, spring 1991, pp. 50-65.

[6] This report will be updated as issues develop and in the event of legislative change. For the most current information about pending legislation, please consult the Legislative Information System (LIS) at http://www.congress.gov.

[7] U.S. Executive Office of the President, Office of Management and Budget, *Analytical Perspectives, Budget of the United States Government, Fiscal Year 2013*, pp. 373-374.

[8] Ibid., p. 374.

[9] For data on the estimated future cost of outstanding credit by program, see **Appendix B**. The number of credit programs depends on the degree of aggregation, and data in **Table B-1** are highly aggregated.

[10] This list of subsidies is paraphrased from the following source, U.S. Executive Office of the President, Office of Management and Budget, *Special Analysis F, Federal Credit Programs, Budget of the United States Government, Fiscal Year 1988* (Washington, DC: GPO, 1987), p. F32.

[11] Ibid., p. F33.

[12] For an explanation of these budget concepts, see *Report of the President's Commission on Budget Concepts* (Washington, DC: GPO, 1967), pp. 82-83.

[13] Ibid., p. 1.

[14] Ibid., p. 105.

[15] Ibid., p. 14.

[16] Ibid., p. 16.

[17] Ibid.

[18] Ibid., p. 18.

[19] The budgetary treatment of federal credit before FY1992 is described in **Appendix C**.

[20] For hypothetical examples of the operation of a direct loan program and a loan guarantee program under the Federal Credit Reform Act of 1990, see **Appendix D** and **Appendix E**.

[21] The derivation of the discount rate was revised by the Balanced Budget Act of 1997.

[22] These transfers within the government represent transfers of budgetary resources rather than actual financial resources.

[23] U.S. Executive Office of the President, Office of Management and Budget, *Analytical Perspectives, Budget of the United States Government, Fiscal Year 2009* (Washington, DC: GPO, 2008), p. 359.

[24] U.S. Executive Office of the President, Office of Management and Budget, *The Budget System and Concepts, Budget of the United States Government, Fiscal Year 2003* (Washington, DC: GPO, 2002), p. 15.

[25] *U.S. Code, Congressional and Administrative News,* 101st Cong., 2nd sess., vol. 6 (St. Paul, MN: West Publishing Co., 1991), pp. 610-615.

[26] David B. Pariser, "Implementing Federal Credit Reform: Challenges Facing Public Sector Financial Manager," *Public Budgeting & Finance*, vol. 12, no. 4, winter 1992, p. 28.

[27] U.S. Executive Office of the President, Office of Management and Budget, *Budget of the United States Government, Fiscal Year 1994* (Washington, DC: GPO, 1993), p. 49.

[28] Ibid.

[29] U.S. Executive Office of the President. Office of Management and Budget, *Policies for Federal Credit Programs and Non-Tax Receivables*, Circular A-129 (Washington, DC: continually updated), p. 27.

[30] OMB's Circulars A-11 and A-129 are available at http://www.whitehouse.gov/omb/circulars.

[31] U.S. Executive Office of the President, Office of Management and Budget, *Analytical Perspectives, Budget of the United States Government, Fiscal Year 2004* (Washington, DC: GPO, 2003), p. 217; and *Analytical Perspectives, Budget of the United States Government, Fiscal Year 2009*, p. 96.

[32] U.S. Executive Office of the President, Office of Management and Budget, *Federal Credit Supplement, Budget of the United States Government, Fiscal Year 1997* (Washington, DC: GPO, 1996), pp. 48-49.
[33] U.S. General Accounting Office, *Credit Reform: Greater Effort Needed to Overcome Persistent Cost Estimation Problems*, Report no. AIMD-98-14 (Washington, DC: GPO, March 1998), pp. 9-10.
[34] Ibid., p. 11.
[35] David Torregrosa, "Credit Subsidy Reestimates, 1993-99," *Public Budgeting & Finance*, vol. 21, no. 2, summer 2001, p. 114. At the time this article was published, the author was an analyst in CBO's Microeconomic and Financial Studies Division.
[36] Marvin Phaup, "Credit Reform, Negative Subsidies, and FHA," *Public Budgeting & Finance*, vol. 16, no. 1, spring 1996, p. 24.
[37] U.S. Executive Office of the President, Office of Management and Budget, *Analytical Perspectives, Budget of the United States Government, Fiscal Year 2007* (Washington, DC, GPO, 2006), p. 390.
[38] Ibid.
[39] For a discussion of the board's conclusions on issues raised by these comments, see U.S. Executive Office of the President, Office of Management and Budget, *Accounting for Direct Loans and Loan Guarantees: Statement of the Federal Financial Accounting Standards*, no. 2 (Washington, DC: August 23, 1993), pp. 21-42.
[40] For a detailed example of the estimation of credit subsidies, see U.S. General Accounting Office, *Credit Subsidy Estimates for the Sections 7(a) and 504 Business Loan Programs*, Report no. T-RCED-97-197 (Washington, DC: GPO, July 16, 1997), p. 19.
[41] U.S. Executive Office of the President, Office of Management and Budget, *Accounting for Direct Loans and Loan Guarantees: Statement of the Federal Financial Accounting Standards,* pp. 21-42.
[42] U.S. Executive Office of the President, Office of Management and Budget, *Analytical Perspectives, Budget of the United States, Fiscal Year 1999* (Washington, DC: GPO, 1998), p. 170.
[43] Ibid.
[44] Ibid.
[45] Ibid.
[46] Ibid.
[47] U.S. Congress, Conference Committee, *Balanced Budget Act of 1997, Conference Report to Accompany H.R. 2015*, H.Rept. 105-217, 105th Cong., 1st sess. (Washington, DC: July 30, 1997), pp. 996-997.
[48] For a comprehensive analysis of this issue, see U.S. Government Accountability Office, *DOE Loan Guarantee Program for Projects That Employ Innovative Technologies*, Report no. GAO-07-339R, February 28, 2007.
[49] U.S. Executive Office of the President, Office of Management and Budget, *Federal Credit Supplement, Budget of the United States Government, Fiscal Year 2013*, pp. 9, 13.
[50] Ibid.
[51] U.S. Executive Office of the President, Office of Management and Budget, *Analytical Perspectives, Budget of the United States Government, Fiscal Year 2013,* pp. 405-406.
[52] Ibid., p. 405. For data on proposed loan levels on each direct loan program, see **Appendix F**.
[53] Ibid., p. 407.
[54] For an overview of FHA loans, see CRS Report RS20530, *FHA-Insured Home Loans: An Overview*, by Katie Jones.
[55] Ibid., For data on proposed loan levels on each loan guarantee program, see **Appendix G**.
[56] Julie Andersen Hill, "Bailouts and Credit Cycles: Fannie, Freddie, and the Farm Credit System," *Wisconsin Law Review*, vol. 2010, no. 1, July 2010, pp. 36-37.
[57] Ibid., pp. 38-42.

[58] CRS Report RS22950, *Fannie Mae and Freddie Mac in Conservatorship*, by Mark Jickling, p. 2.

[59] CRS Report R41822, *Proposals to Reform Fannie Mae and Freddie Mac in the 112th Congress*, by N. Eric Weiss.

[60] For a comprehensive analysis of the current budgetary treatment of a federal insurance program, see Congressional Budget Office, *The Budgetary Treatment of Subsidies in the National Flood Insurance Program*, Testimony of Donald B. Marron, Acting Director, before the Senate Committee on Banking, Housing, and Urban Affairs, January 25, 2006.

[61] U.S. General Accounting Office, *Budget Issues: Budgeting for Federal Insurance Programs*, Report no. AIMD-97-16 (Washington, DC: September 1997), p. 6.

[62] Ibid., p. 7.

[63] U.S. General Accounting Office, *Budget Issues: Budgeting for Federal Insurance Programs*, Testimony before the Budget Task Force, Committee on the Budget, House of Representatives, Report no. T-AIMD-98-147 (Washington, DC, April 23, 1998), p. 9.

[64] Ibid.

[65] Ibid., p. 13.

[66] U.S. General Accounting Office, *Budget Issues: Budgeting for Federal Insurance Programs*, Report no. AIMD-97-16, p. 10.

[67] U.S,. General Accounting Office, *Budget Process: Extending Budget Controls*, Testimony of Susan J. Irving, Director, Federal Budget Analysis, before the House Committee on the Budget, April 26, 2002, p. 16.

[68] This change would require new legislation because the FCRA specifies that the subsidy cost of federal credit is the cost to the taxpayer rather than the market value to the recipient.

[69] U.S. General Accounting Office, *Budgetary Treatment of Federal Credit Programs*, Report No. AFMD-89-42 (Washington, DC, April 1989), p. 28.

[70] Ibid., p. 3.

[71] Ibid., p. 7.

[72] For a detailed explanation of options, see CRS Report R40646, *Derivatives Regulation and Legislation Through the 111th Congress*, by Rena S. Miller, p. 27.

[73] Congressional Budget Office, Estimating the Value of Subsidies for Federal Loans and Loan Guarantees, August 2004, p. 8.

[74] Ibid.

[75] Ibid.

[76] Ibid.

[77] Ibid., p. 9.

[78] Ibid., pp. 12-19.

[79] Ibid.

[80] U.S. Executive Office of the President, Office of Management and Budget, *Analytical Perspectives, Budget of the U.S. Government, Fiscal Year 2013* (Washington, DC: GPO. 2012), pp. 393-399.

[81] Congressional Budget Office, *Fair-Value Accounting for Federal Credit Programs*, March 2012.

[82] Ibid., p. 3.

[83] Congressional Budget Office, *Fair-Value Accounting for Federal Credit Programs*, p. 5.

[84] Ibid.

[85] For a comprehensive analysis of the debate over the inclusion of market risk, see CRS Report R42503, *Subsidy Cost of Federal Credit: Cost to the Government or Fair Value Cost?*, by James M. Bickley.

[86] Congressional Budget Office, *Fair-Value Accounting for Federal Credit* Programs, pp. 10-11.

[87] In addition, House Fiscal Year 2012 Budget Resolution (H.Con.Res. 34, 112th Congress) and House Fiscal Year 2013 Budget Resolution (H.Con.Res. 112, 112th Congress) have provisions for the calculation of subsidy costs using fair value accounting.

[88] Section 501(1).

[89] Section 502(7)(A).
[90] Section 504(a).
[91] Section 502(5)(A).
[92] Section 504(g).
[93] For action by the House Budget Committee, see H.Rept. 112-380, Part 1.
[94] Section 501(1).
[95] Section 502(5)(A).
[96] Section 201.
[97] Section 202.
[98] This appendix is an edited excerpt from the following website: http://www.accounting 4management.com/ concept_of_present_value.htm.
[99] U.S. Executive Office of the President, Office of Management and Budget, *Special Analysis F, Federal Credit Programs, Budget of the United States Government, Fiscal Year 1990* (Washington, DC: GPO, 1989), p. F4.
[100] The estimated appropriation acts limitation on credit loan levels by program are published annually in the Analytical Perspectives, Budget of the United States.
[101] If program L is a mandatory loan program, an automatic appropriation of budget authority to cover the estimated subsidy costs would occur for whatever amount of credit is needed to meet the estimated demand for services by beneficiaries.
[102] If program G is a mandatory loan guarantee program, an automatic appropriation of budget authority would occur for whatever amount of credit needed to meet the estimated demand for services by beneficiaries.

In: Federal Credit
Editor: Ethan A. Kelly

ISBN: 978-1-62417-553-4


*Chapter 2*

# SUBSIDY COST OF FEDERAL CREDIT: COST TO THE GOVERNMENT OR FAIR VALUE COST?*

*James M. Bickley*

## SUMMARY

Since the mid-1980s, budget experts have debated whether the best method of measuring the subsidy cost of federal credit (direct loans and loan guarantees) is the cost to the government or the fair value cost. The cost to the government would reflect the actual budget cost measured by discounting of expected cash flows associated with each program at the interest rate on risk-free Treasury securities. The measure of the cost to the government would place the cost of federal credit on the same basis as a grant or a tax expenditure; consequently, policymakers would have an incentive to use the most appropriate means to cover the cost of a government program.

The fair value cost would equal the cost that the credit recipient would have had to pay to borrow on the private credit market. The fair value cost would include market risk and reflect the opportunity cost of shifting capital from the private sector to the public sector. Proponents argue that the social

* This is an edited, reformatted and augmented version of the Congressional Research Service Publication, CRS Report for Congress R42503, dated April 25, 2012.

cost rather than the budgetary cost should be used to allocate resources between the public and private sectors. This debate has yet to be resolved.

The U.S. government uses federal credit to allocate financial capital to a range of areas, including home ownership, student loans, small business, agriculture, and energy. A direct loan is a disbursement of funds by the government to a nonfederal borrower under a contract that requires the repayment of such funds with or without interest. A loan guarantee is a pledge by the federal government to repay all or part of the principal or interest on any debt obligation of a non-federal borrower to a non-federal lender. At the end of FY2011, outstanding federal direct loans totaled $838 billion and outstanding guaranteed loans totaled $2,017 billion.

Before FY1992, federal credit programs were measured on an annual cash flow basis. A new federal direct loan was treated as a budget outlay in the current fiscal year, and repayments of principal and payments of interest were treated as offsetting collections (negative outlays) in the future fiscal years in which they occurred. In the year it was granted, a loan guarantee was a contingent liability, which means the federal government was only responsible for repayment in the event of a default. Congress and the executive branch debated options to convert the budgetary treatment of federal credit from cash flow accounting to accrual accounting, which would record the subsidy cost of federal credit over the entire life of a loan or loan guarantee. One of the primary decisions concerning accrual accounting was whether the subsidy cost of federal credit should be measured by the "cost to the government" or the "fair value" cost.

On November 5, 1990, the President signed P.L. 101-508, 104 Stat. 1388, the Omnibus Budget Reconciliation Act of 1990 (OBRA90), which included the Federal Credit Reform Act of 1990 (FCRA). Beginning with FY1992, FCRA changed the methodology in the unified budget for measuring and reporting the cost of federal direct loans and federal loan guarantees from cash flow to accrual accounting with the cost to the government used in measuring subsidy costs.

In the 112$^{th}$ Congress, six bills have been introduced that would provide for calculation of subsidy costs using fair value accounting: companion bills S. 1651/H.R. 3414 (Honest Budget Act), H.R. 3581 (Budget and Accounting Transparency Act of 2011), H.R. 3844 (Honest Budget Act of 2012), House Fiscal Year 2012 Budget Resolution (H.Con.Res. 34, 112$^{th}$ Congress), and House Fiscal Year 2013 Budget Resolution (H.Con.Res. 112, 112$^{th}$ Congress). This report presents a chronology of this still unresolved debate, which dates from the mid-1980s.

# INTRODUCTION

Since the mid-1980s, budget experts have debated whether the best method of measuring the subsidy cost of federal credit (direct loans or loan guarantees) is the cost to the government or the fair value cost. Federal credit is direct loans and loan guarantees. The cost to the government would reflect the actual budget cost measured by discounting of expected cash flows associated with each program at the interest rate on risk-free Treasury securities. The measure of the cost to the government would place the cost of federal credit on the same basis as a grant or a tax expenditure; consequently, policymakers would have an incentive to use the most appropriate means to cover the cost of a government program.

The fair value cost estimate would equal the cost that the credit recipient would have had to pay to borrow on the private credit market. The fair value cost estimate would include market risk and reflect the opportunity cost of shifting capital from the private sector to the public sector, thus reflecting the social cost of the programs. Proponents argue that the social cost rather than the budgetary cost should be used to allocate resources between the public and private sectors. This debate has yet to be resolved.

The U.S. government uses federal credit to allocate financial capital to a range of areas including home ownership, student loans, small business, agriculture, and energy.[1] A direct loan is "a disbursement of funds by the government to a nonfederal borrower under a contract that requires the repayment of such funds with or without interest."[2] A loan guarantee is "a pledge with respect to the payment of all or part of the principal or interest on any debt obligation of a non-federal borrower to a non-federal lender."[3] At the end of FY2011, outstanding federal direct loans totaled $838 billion and outstanding guaranteed loans totaled $2,017 billion.[4] Thus, at the end of FY2011, outstanding federal credit totaled $2.855 trillion.

The weak economy and expansionary monetary policy caused low nominal Treasury interest rates from FY2009 to FY2011. Consequently, the use of Treasury interest rates in the cost-to-the-government measure resulted in aggregate costs of federal credit of negative $19 billion for FY2009, negative $20 billion for FY2010, and negative $41 billion for FY2011.[5] These negative costs reduced the sizes of the federal deficits. In contrast, the aggregate cost of federal credit averaged $3.1 billion annually for FY1998-FY2008.[6] Arguably, these negative aggregate costs of federal credit over the past three fiscal years have contributed to the debate about changing to fair value budgeting. In the 112th Congress, six bills have been introduced that would provide for calculation of subsidy costs using fair value accounting: companion bills S. 1651/H.R. 3414 (Honest Budget Act), H.R. 3581 (Budget and Accounting Transparency Act of 2011), H.R. 3844 (Honest Budget Act of 2012), House Fiscal Year 2012 Budget Resolution (H.Con.Res. 34, 112th Congress), and House Fiscal Year 2013 Budget Resolution (H.Con.Res. 112, 112th Congress).

Before FY1992, federal credit programs were measured on an annual cash flow basis. Under this arrangement, a new federal direct loan was treated as a budget outlay in the current fiscal year, and repayments of principal and payments of interest were treated as offsetting collections (negative outlays) in the fiscal years in which they were repaid. If a loan recipient paid a fee, this fee was also treated as an offsetting collection. Loan defaults reduced repayments of principal and interest, and therefore offsetting collections. Administrative expenses were reported as outlays. In a given fiscal year, the budgetary cost of a loan program, not the individual loans, was its net cash flow. This equaled new loans made plus any administrative expenses associated with these loans (rarely recognized in the loan accounts) less any loan fees, repayments of principal, and payments of interest. The federal acceptance of a contingent liability when a loan guarantee was provided was not included in the federal budget because no cash flow occurred. The administrative costs of a guarantee program were outlays in the fiscal year in which they occurred.

Some guarantee programs charge fees to the recipient, and these fees were considered offsetting collections. Any federal outlays necessary to compensate lenders for any default losses covered by a federal guarantee were not shown in the budget until they were actually paid.

Using the old cash-flow method, it was often difficult for policymakers to accurately monitor and therefore make informed decisions about federal credit. In addition, administrators at agencies could understate costs by using various budgetary techniques. One of these was generating “savings” from the fees on increased volumes of new guarantees while ignoring the increase in expected losses and offsetting the (cash) cost of new direct loans with current year collections from old loans.

To remedy these problems, Congress and the executive branch debated options to convert the budgetary treatment of federal credit from cash flow accounting to accrual accounting (measuring the cost over the life of the loan or loan guarantee). One of the primary decisions concerned whether the cost of federal credit should be measured by the “cost to the government” or the “fair value” cost.

## "Cost to the Government"

The cost to the government approach reflects the actual budget cost measured by "discounting of expected cash flows at the interest rate on risk-free Treasury securities (the rate at which the government borrows money)."[7] For a loan program, these credit flows consist of "disbursements by the government (loan disbursement and other payments) minus estimated payments to the government (repayment of principal, payments of interest, and other payments) after adjusting for projected defaults, prepayments, fees, penalties, and other recoveries."[8] For a loan guarantee program, these credit flows are "estimated payments by the government (for defaults and delinquencies, interest rate subsidies, and other payments) minus estimated payment to the government (for loan origination and other fees, penalties, and recoveries)."[9]

The cost to the government concept would measure the subsidy cost in an equivalent budgetary method for a grant or a tax expenditure. Thus, a policymaker would not have any incentive to favor one type of assistance over another because credit, grants, and tax expenditures would all be measured by the cost to the government.

## "Fair Value Cost"

An alternative would be to use the fair value cost, which would equal the cost that the credit recipient would have had to pay to borrow on the private credit market. In other words, the fair value cost is based on the price investors would be willing to pay to purchase federal direct loan assets or reinsure federal loan guarantees. The fair value cost includes market risk and reflects the opportunity cost of shifting capital from the private sector to the public sector.

On November 5, 1990, President George H. W. Bush signed P.L. 101-508, 104 Stat. 1388, the Omnibus Budget Reconciliation Act of 1990 (OBRA90). The legislation added a new title to the Congressional Budget Act, Title V, the Federal Credit Reform Act of 1990 (FCRA). Beginning with FY1992, FCRA changed the methodology in the unified budget for measuring and reporting the cost of federal direct loans and federal loan guarantees from cash flow to accrual accounting, using the cost to the government concept. Whether the cost to the government or the fair value cost is most appropriate is still debated, however, and the question remains unresolved. This report gives a chronological examination of this debate since the 1980s.

## DEBATE IN MID-1980S

In August 1984, the Office of Management and Budget (OMB) issued a revised version of its Circular A-70, *Policies and Guidelines for Federal Credit Programs*, which included the requirement that federal agencies calculate and transmit data to OMB on the subsidy cost of all of their direct loan and loan guarantee programs. The method used to measure subsidy costs was specified as comparing private financing terms with those of federal credit. Since 1984, these agency data were used to report subsidy costs in Special Analysis F, "Federal Credit Programs," in the President's budget documents.[10]

On December 12, 1985, the passage of the Gramm-Rudman-Hollings (G-R-H) Act, Balanced Budget and Emergency Deficit Control Act of 1985 (P.L. 99-177), 99 Stat. 1037, required that all new direct loans and loan guarantees be on-budget.[11] Prior to G-R-H, many new direct loans and loan guarantees were recorded off-budget. With the passage of G-R-H, Congress and the executive branch became more interested in possible budgetary reforms to improve the recording of federal credit in the budget. One of the major issues was measuring the subsidy costs of federal credit. This new interest prompted both proposed legislation and research in legislative and executive branch agencies and the academic community.

## PROPOSED CREDIT REFORM LEGISLATION IN 1987

In February 1987, the Reagan Administration proposed extensive credit reform in its FY1988 Budget.[12] The Administration's proposals were introduced in the House as H.R. 1754 and the Senate as S. 745, the Federal Credit Reform Act of 1987. Senators Lawton Chiles and Pete Domenici extensively revised the Reagan proposal. Their proposal was included as an amendment to H.J.Res. 324 to raise the debt limit as it passed the Senate on July 31, 1987, but was eliminated by the conference agreement.[13]

The Administration's proposal measured the subsidy cost as the dollar benefit to the borrower, while the Chiles-Domenici proposal measured subsidy cost as the dollar cost to the federal government. Furthermore, the two proposals differed in their methods of determining the value of subsidy costs.

The Administration proposed to sell most loans on private credit markets.[14] The value of a loan's subsidy cost would equal the difference between its face value and its selling price. The Administration's proposal also sought to reinsure most loan guarantees with single payment policies, and government's payment for reinsurance would measure the subsidy cost. Thus, most credit subsidies would be measured objectively by market forces. For those credit programs for which loan sales and guarantee reinsurance would be inappropriate, the subsidy cost was to be estimated by the Secretary of the Treasury in consultation with the relevant agencies.

The Chiles-Domenici proposal neither required nor authorized the selling of direct loans and specifically forbade the reinsurance of federal loan guarantees. These stipulations reflected the belief that market transactions would have been inappropriate in measuring the subsidy cost to the federal government. Under the Chiles-Domenici proposal, a federal credit management agency would have been established in the Treasury Department, and this agency would estimate subsidy costs as cost to the government.

## GAO's 1989 Report

In April 1989, the then-General Accounting Office issued a report titled *Budgetary Treatment of Federal Credit Programs*, which included analyses of credit reform proposals recommended by the Senate Budget Committee, CBO, OMB, and GAO.[15] In the report, GAO stated the following:

> The four proposals differ principally only on the method used to calculate credit subsidy costs. We [GAO] and the Senate Budget Committee propose measuring the direct budgetary costs of credit programs. In our recent reports, we recommend a "cost-to-the-government" model, which measures loan subsidy costs as the difference between the costs to the Treasury of making the loan and the expected receipts flowing back to the Treasury from the loan repayments—calculated on a present-value basis.
>
> On the other hand, CBO and OMB prefer a market-valuation oriented measurement approach which calculates the economic benefit borrowers receive as a result of obtaining federal, rather than private sector, loans. OMB believes that the economic subsidy offered to borrowers is the most important aspect of federal credit, and it proposes

> putting this economic subsidy measure in the federal budget. OMB computes subsidy costs as the present value of the additional payments that a federal borrower would be required to pay for a similar loan from the private sector. CBO's preference for market-valuation subsidy costs is based on the assumption that government credit program costs appropriately measured are comparable to costs incurred by private sector financial institutions.
>
> As stated in our prior reports, we [GAO] prefer the cost-to-the-government measure of credit subsidy costs because it measures future cash outlays. We believe that market-valuation subsidy costs will overstate the actual cost to the government. Subsidies measured in terms of market values will generally be larger than subsidies measured in terms of the cost to the government because they will include some costs, such as premiums for liquidity and risk (above and beyond expected default costs), which would not be reflected in budget outlays.[16]

## CBO's 1989 Report

In December 1989, the Congressional Budget Office (CBO) published a report titled *Credit Reform: Comparable Budget Costs for Cash and Credit*, which provided an analysis of federal credit reform proposals.[17] One chapter explained possible methods of calculating subsidy costs of federal credit,[18] and discussed selecting the appropriate discount rate in determining costs. In examining the option of using Treasury borrowing rates, the report stated the following:

> The bills, notes, and bonds issued by the Treasury are believed to be virtually free of default risk. Rates on such debt, therefore, contain no risk premium and are commonly considered risk-free. Use of a Treasury borrowing rate to discount future cash flows on a credit contract treats those payments as though they were certain to be received. If the government were to use its own risk-free cost of borrowing to discount uncertain future cash flows, it would be the only financial institution to do so. An aversion to risk causes others, including federally insured banks and thrifts, to discount risky income at a higher than risk-free rate.
>
> Those who recommend that the government use a risk-free rate to discount risky future income argue that the risk-free rate reflects what the government actually pays to provide credit assistance. GAO, for example, has advocated valuing federal loans by using Treasury borrowing rates to discount receipts, minus losses from defaults. Using a risk-free Treasury rate for discounting supports a budget policy that recognizes only costs paid in cash.[19]

The report also considered the option of using market rates:

> Others recommend that the government select a discount rate equal to the rate that the government would receive by investing in other equally risky assets. They maintain that the use of such a rate is necessary to capture the opportunity costs of credit or the value of alternatives forgone. The use of rates that account for risk is also necessary to distinguish the cost of assets with equal expected income but different degrees of risk.[20]

The report indicated major data deficiencies in making subsidy cost calculations. "In general, federal agencies do not have access to historical data on the characteristics of borrowers, on the financed project, or on the cash flows for individual loans and guarantees."[21]

## FEDERAL CREDIT REFORM ACT OF 1990

On November 5, 1990, the President signed P.L. 101-508, 104 Stat. 1388, the Omnibus Budget Reconciliation Act of 1990 (OBRA90). The legislation added a new title to the Congressional Budget Act, Title V, the Federal Credit Reform Act of 1990 (FCRA). Beginning with FY1992, FCRA changed the methodology in the unified budget for measuring and reporting the cost of federal direct loans and federal loan guarantees from cash flow to accrual accounting.

The four stated purposes of FCRA (Section 501) were to

(1) measure more accurately the costs of federal credit programs;
(2) place the cost of credit programs on a budgetary basis equivalent to other federal spending;
(3) encourage the delivery of benefits in the form most appropriate to the needs of beneficiaries; and
(4) improve the allocation of resources among credit programs and other spending.

FCRA required the budgetary cost of federal credit to be measured for any one year as the net present value of the cost to the government of credit subsidies in the fiscal year the credit is provided.

Although FCRA specified the use of the cost to the taxpayer in measuring credit subsidies, some public finance professionals, including some experts at CBO, continued to advocate a shift to the use of fair value cost.

## CBO's 2004 Report

In August 2004, CBO issued a report on federal credit subsidies that examined two ways of including the market price for risk: risk-adjusted discount rates and options-pricing methods.[22]

The risk-adjusted discount rate (ADR) method "adds a spread—the difference between the interest rate on a Treasury security and the rate on a risky security—to Treasury rates and uses the resulting adjusted rate to discount expected cash flows associated with a loan."[23] The ADR method results in a higher discount rate for both costs and revenues and, with a few exceptions for negative subsidies, raises the net cost of credit programs.

"An option is a marketable security which allows the owner to buy (or sell) another security at a stipulated price on or before a specified date."[24] " The general ideal behind options-pricing methods is that assets with the same payoffs must have the same price; otherwise, investors would have the opportunity to earn a risk-free profit by buying low and selling high."[25] An options-pricing method is likely to be more accurate than the ADR method, but only when the necessary data and model are available.[26]

Options-pricing models are seldom used to value credit provided to individuals; instead the use of the ADR method is usually appropriate.[27] Option-pricing methods are usually better than ADR methods in valuing credit provided to commercial enterprises.[28] The best method to use varies for other credit programs, such as "loan assistance to sovereign states, municipalities, and special-purpose enterprises."[29]

As an example of the process, CBO applied a type of options pricing—the binomial pricing method—to calculate the risk-adjusted cost of extending federal loan guarantees to Chrysler in 1980 and to America West Airlines (AWA) in 2002. CBO computed that the market-value loss of the Chrysler loan guarantee was $239.0 million instead of the Treasury-rate loss of $107.6 million.[30]

CBO also found that the calculated market-value loss was $26.3 million for the AWA loan guarantee instead of a gain of $47.4 million using Treasury interest rates.[31]

## President's 2010 Fiscal Commission

In 2010, President Barack Obama established the National Commission on Fiscal Responsibility and Reform "to address the nation's fiscal challenges."[32] In December 2010, the commission issued its report that included a recommendation to "Review and Reform Budget Concepts." This recommendation stated that

> Current scoring rules and definitions cause policy makers to undervalue some policies and overvalue others. The Commission recommends a complete review of all budget scoring practices ("budget concepts") by the budget committees, the Congressional Budget Office, and the Office of Management and Budget. Changes should aim to more accurately reflect the true cost of government liabilities, including by considering accrual accounting, risk-adjusted credit reforms, and similar concepts.[33]

Thus, the President's fiscal commission arguably endorsed considering a change to fair value accounting for credit programs.

## House FY2012 Budget Resolution

On April 11, 2011, Representative Paul Ryan, chairman of the House Committee on the Budget, introduced the Fiscal Year 2012 Budget Resolution, H.Con.Res. 34, 112th Congress. This resolution passed the House by a yeas to nays vote of 235 to 193 but was rejected in the Senate by a yeas to nays vote of 40 to 57.

Section 408, "Fair Value Estimates," requires that any CBO estimate prepared for a measure under the Federal Credit Reform Act shall also provide, as a supplement, and to the extent practicable, upon the request of the chairman or ranking Member of the Committee on the Budget, an estimate of the current actual or estimated market values representing the "fair value" of assets and liabilities affected by such measure.

Section 408 also authorizes the chairman to use such estimate to determine compliance with the Congressional Budget Act of 1974 and other budgetary enforcement controls. Thus, this budget resolution was supportive of fair value accounting.

## Budget and Accounting Transparency Act of 2011

On December 7, 2011, Representative Scott Garrett introduced H.R. 3581, the Budget and Accounting Transparency Act of 2011.[34]

On February 7, 2012, the House passed H.R. 3581 by a yeas to nays vote of 245 to 180.

On February 9, 2012, the act was referred to the Senate Committee on the Budget. This act includes a provision that would amend FCRA by requiring the calculation of the subsidy cost of federal credit be accounted for on a "fair value" basis.

## Report of the Center on Budget and Policy Priorities, 2012

On January 24, 2012, the Center on Budget and Policy Priorities (CBPP)[35] issued a report opposing H.R. 3581 titled *House Bill Would Artificially Inflate Cost of Federal Credit Programs*.[36]

The authors argue that the addition of a risk component would overstate the federal costs of credit programs and force policy makers to offset phantom costs with phantom offsets in order to avoid overstating the size of the federal deficit.[37] The authors maintain that H.R. 3581 has "the four flaws," alleged negative characteristics that are identified below.

### CBPP Criticism of H.R. 3581

- *Government May Be Less Risk Averse than Individuals*

  The authors argue that "individuals are risk averse in part because their financial assets are likely to be needed at specific times, even when the value of those assets has declined."[38] In contrast, the Treasury can borrow inexpensively when the times are bad.

- *Risk Aversion Is Not a Budgetary Cost*

  The authors assert that "adding a risk-aversion adjustment to the spending side of the budget would add an extra 'cost' that the government does not actually incur—and that doesn't need to be covered by additional taxes or borrowing."[39] Thus, a risk-aversion adjustment would be a *phantom cost.*[40]

- *Proposal Does Not Treat All Programs the Same*

The authors maintain that "when allocating public funds, the budget must reflect costs comparable across all programs."[41] But the Budget and Accounting Transparency Act of 2011 "would make credit programs appear more expensive to the Treasury than they truly are without making similar adjustment for other programs whose actual costs also are uncertain."[42]

- *Phantom Costs Require Phantom Offsets*

The authors declare that the phantom cost from the risk-aversion adjustment causes proponents "to tacitly or explicitly advocate accompanying that adjustment with a *phantom offset.*"[43] The authors state that the Budget and Accounting Transparency Act of 2011

> creates a phantom downward "means of financing" offset that, over time, would prevent the debt from being too high even though the annual deficits would consistently be overstated. One result of this approach is that the sum of deficits over time would diverge more than it already does from the amount of debt held by the public.[44]

Although the authors believe that a risk-aversion cost should not play a part in budget accounting, it "should play a part in the *cost-benefit analysis* that policymakers should undertake in deciding whether a government program constitutes wise public policy."[45] Furthermore, in response to a request from Representative Chris Van Hollen, Robert D. Reischauer, a member of the CBPP board of directors and president emeritus of the Urban Institute, sent a letter expressing his strong opposition to the use of fair value accounting in proposed H.R. 3581. He stated that

> H.R. 3581 proposes to place an additional budgetary cost on top of the actual cash flows. This additional cost is supposed to reflect a cost to society that stems from the fact that, even if the cash flows turn out to be exactly as estimated, the *possibility* that the credit programs would cost more (or Less) than estimated imposes a cost on a risk-averse public.[46]

## Criticism of CBPP Report by Phaup

Professor Marvin Phaup, a research scholar and professorial lecturer at the Trachtenberg School of Public Administration and Public Policy at George Washington University, wrote a comment on CBPP's release on H.R. 3581.[47] Professor Phaup made the following five points:[48]

- H.R. 3581, he asserted, would remove "phantom" budgetary gains to the government from direct lending and loan guarantee programs. Those illusory gains mislead policy makers about the costs of their policy decisions.
- What he described as illusory gains on federal credit also encourage budget gimmickry. For example, FCRTA would permit the government to balance its budget immediately on paper by issuing large amounts of Treasury debt and using the proceeds to invest in an equally large portfolio of risky loans.

  In his view, this result would be absurd because in issuing a dollar of debt and buying a dollar of risky loans at market prices, the government's net financial position is unchanged.
- According to Professor Phaup, if the current practice of using the prices of Treasury securities to value risky loans rather than the market value of the risky securities themselves were extended to other assets, then the government could—with the same logic—direct the Treasury to buy a ton of lead, value it at the price of gold, and record the gain as deficit reduction.
- The cost of market risk, he maintains, should be a budget cost because it is a cost to government stakeholders and its absorption by some yields an unrecognized subsidy to others.

  CBPP would include this cost in cost-benefit analyses where the purpose is to decide if a federal activity produces a net gain but not in the budget. Budgeting without an evaluation function, however, he considers to belittle more than a redundant projection of Treasury's borrowing requirements.
- Finally, he suggests that the cost of market risk should not be excluded from the budget on grounds that the money isn't paid out by the government. Both the Universal Service Fund and the United Mine Workers of American Benefit Funds are included in the budget, even though the money is untouched by federal hands.

# Analysis of Fair Value Budgeting in FY2013 Budget

In the President's Budget for FY2013, the Office of Management and Budget selected "Fair Value Budgeting for Credit Programs" as a topic for in-depth analysis.[49]

OMB compared and contrasted the current cost to the government with fair value budgeting, which would reflect social costs. OMB found that

> The current FCRA method for estimating cost provides a different measure of cost than the fair value method, which takes different risks and costs into account. To calculate fair value, cash flows unadjusted for expected losses would be discounted with a market rate that reflects the characters of the cash flows of the loan or loan guarantee (comparable market rate), instead of Treasury rates. The comparable market rate would differ from the maturity-matched Treasury rate in most cases and vary across credit programs, and even across individual loans and guarantees in some cases.
>
> Fair value is conceptually appealing in that it reflects closely the preferences of market participants. It is debatable, however, whether fair value estimates for credit programs also represent the preferences of taxpayers and the society as a whole. In addition to this conceptual issue, several practical and implementation issues would need to be carefully considered in evaluating fair value proposals. Key issues include: how to develop accurate estimation methods; comparability of cost estimates across programs; and whether agencies would be able to implement fair value, particularly given limited administrative resources. A fair value proposal that does not address these conceptual and practical issues would probably fail to improve resource allocation and could even be counter-productive.[50]

OMB stated that the market interest rate on a private loan depends on seven factors, with only the first two of the following being reflected in the Treasury rate.[51] These seven factors were identified by OMB:

- time preference (present versus future, included in FCRA cost estimate)
- expected loss from default (included in FCRA cost estimate)
- compensation for uncertain returns—uncertainty premium
- compensation for lower liquidity—liquidity premium

- cost of administering the loan (This cost is not included in an FCRA cost estimate but is relevant to taxpayers. It is currently recorded on a cash basis.)
- tax rate on interest income
- contract terms determining lenders' and borrowers' rights

## CBO Issue Brief on Fair-Value Accounting

In March 2012, CBO released an issue brief titled *Fair-Value Accounting for Federal Credit Programs*. CBO indicated its support for fair value accounting:

> FCRA cost estimates understate the cost of federal credit programs to the government because of the requirement that Treasury rates be used for discounting. Using comprehensive cost measures for budgeting, and accounting for credit on a basis that is equivalent to that for other federal programs—stated objectives of FCRA—would be better accomplished if the cost of extending federal credit was assessed at market prices rather than on a FCRA basis.[52]

CBO acknowledges that fair value accounting involves implementation issues. "Because most public-sector credit programs have no exact analogue in the private sector, estimating their fair value usually involves approximation."[53] Fair value accounting would result in additional effort and expense.[54] Fair value estimates would be more volatile "over time because the cost of market risk is not constant."[55] Finally, "fair-value estimates might be less transparent than FCRA estimates and thus more dependent on the judgment of agencies and analysts responsible for the programs."[56] CBO maintains that these concerns, however, can "be addressed in various ways."[57] For example, expert advice from private-sector accounting firms with experience in fair-value accounting could lessen the volatility of estimates, and the establishment of federal guidelines for estimation procedures could make estimates more transparent.[58]

CBO indicates the fair-value accounting is currently applied in a few cases. For example, the Emergency Economic Stabilization Act of 2008 (P.L. 110-343), 122 Stat. 3765, specified that the estimated cost of the Troubled Assist Relief Program be calculated using a discount rate adjusted for the market cost of risk.[59] CBO also has made studies for Congress about the cost of some federal credit programs using fair value account versus the current cost to the government under FCRA.[60]

CBO states that under FCRA, the total subsidy cost of federal credit averaged $3.1 billion annually from FY1998 to FY2008.[61] But the total subsidy cost of federal credit was negative $19 billion for FY2009, negative $20 billion for FY2010, and negative $41 billion for FY2011.[62] These data suggest that a change to fair value accounting could significantly affect the deficit.

## HOUSE FY2013 BUDGET RESOLUTION

On March 23, 2012, Representative Paul Ryan introduced the Fiscal Year 2013 Budget Resolution, H.Con.Res. 112, 112th Congress. The fair value provision was similar to that in the House FY2012 Budget Resolution. On March 29, this budget resolution passed the House by a 228 to 191 vote. Section 507(a) titled "Fair Value Estimates"

> requires the Congressional Budget Office, upon the request of the chair or ranking member of the Committee on the Budget, to make a supplemental estimate of the current actual or estimated market values representing the "fair value" of assets and liabilities affected by a measure as part of any estimate prepared for the measure under credit reform requirements of the Federal Credit Reform Act.
>
> Authorizes the chair to use such estimate to determine compliance of the measure in question with the Congressional Budget Act of 1974 and other budgetary enforcement controls.[63]

Debate about fair value budgeting has yet to be resolved.

## End Notes

[1] For an overview of federal credit reform, see CRS Report RL30346, *Federal Credit Reform: Implementation of the Changed Budgetary Treatment of Direct Loans and Loan Guarantees*, by James M. Bickley.

[2] Section 502(1) of the Federal Credit Reform Act of 1990.

[3] Section 502(3) of the Federal Credit Reform Act of 1990.

[4] U.S. Office of Management and Budget, *Analytical Perspectives, Fiscal Year 2013, Budget of the U.S. Government*, Washington: GPO, 2012), p. 401.

[5] Congressional Budget Office, *Fair-Value Accounting for Federal Credit Programs*, March 2012, p. 5.

[6] Ibid.

[7] Congressional Budget Office, *Estimating the Value of Subsidies for Federal Loans and Loan Guarantees*, August 2004, p. 4.

[8] U.S. Government Accountability Office, *Credit Reform; Review of OMB's Credit Subsidy Model*, Report no.GAO/AIMD-97-145, August 1997, p. 4.

[9] Ibid.

[10] Congress of the United States, Congressional Budget Office, *Credit Reform: Comparable Budget Costs for Cash and Credit*, December 1989, p. 21.

[11] Off-budget accounts are designated by law as excluded from the budget totals. For example, under current law, transactions of the Social Security trust funds and the Postal Service are off-budget. On-budget accounts are other than those designated by law as off-budget. The budget combines the on- and off-budget totals to derive unified totals for federal activity.

[12] The information in this section is from the following source: archived CRS Report 87-939 E, *Credit Reform: Chiles-Domenici Proposal Contrasted with Reagan Proposal*, by James M. Bickley. A copy of this report is available from the author.

[13] For explanations of these proposals, see Executive Office of the President, Office of Management and Budget, *Section-By-Section Analysis of the Federal Credit Reform Act of 1987*, Washington, March 1987, 17 p.; and U.S. Congress, House, *Increasing the Statutory Limit on the Public Debt*, Conference Report to Accompany H.J.Res. 324, 100th Congress, 1st Session, Washington, September 21, 1987, pp. 68-70.

[14] For GAO's views on the federal government's proposed sale of loan assets, see Frederick D. Wolf, "Federal Government Credit Program: Privatization Through Loan Sales," *Public Budgeting & Finance*, vol. 8, no. 4, Winter 1988, pp. 74-80.

[15] U.S. General Accounting Office, *Budgetary Treatment of Federal Credit Programs*, Report No. AFMD-89-42, April 1989, 28 pp.

[16] Ibid., pp. 3-4.

[17] This report satisfied the requirements of Section 212 of the *Balanced Budget and Emergency Deficit Control Reaffirmation Act of 1987* (P.L. 100-119), 101 Stat. 754, which directed CBO in consultation with GAO to study specified aspects of federal credit.

[18] Congressional Budget Office, *Credit Reform: Comparable Budget Costs for Cash and* Credit, pp. 33-46.

[19] Ibid., pp. 39-40.

[20] Ibid., p. 40.

[21] Ibid., p. 36.

[22] Congressional Budget Office, *Estimating the Value of Subsidies for Federal Loans and Loan Guarantees*, August, 2004, p. 4.

[23] Ibid., p. 7.

[24] Robert C. Radcliffe, *Investment: Concepts, Analysis, and Strategy* (Glenview, Ill.: Scott, Foresman and Company, 1982), p. 348.

[25] Congressional Budget Office, *Estimating the Value of Subsidies for Federal Loans and Loan Guarantees*, p. 8.

[26] Ibid.

[27] Ibid.

[28] Ibid.

[29] Ibid., p. 9.

[30] Ibid., pp. 12-19.

[31] Ibid.

[32] The National Commission on Fiscal Responsibility and Reform, *The Moment of Truth*, Washington, December 2010, 65 p.

[33] Ibid., pp. 57-58.

[34] The provisions concerning fair value account in S. 1651, H.R. 3414, and H.R. 3844 were similar to H.R. 3581, but only H.R. 3581 has seen floor action.

[35] The conservative Heritage Foundation refers to the Center on Budget and Policy Priorities as a "liberal" think tank.
[36] Jim Horney, Richard Kogan, and Paul Van de Water, *House Bill Would Artificially Inflate Cost of Federal Credit Programs*, Center on Budget and Policy Priorities, Washington, January 24, 2012, 9 p.
[37] Ibid., p. 1.
[38] Ibid., p. 6.
[39] Ibid.
[40] Ibid.
[41] Ibid., p. 7.
[42] Ibid.
[43] Ibid.
[44] Ibid., p. 8.
[45] Ibid.
[46] Center on Budget and Policy Priorities, "Reischauer 'Strongly Opposes' House Bill to Inflate Cost of Federal Credit Programs," Robert D. Reischauer letter to Representative Chris Van Hollen, January 24, 2012.
[47] Marvin Phaup, *Fair Market Values and the Budgetary Treatment of Federal Credit: Comment on CBPP's Release on H.R. 3581*, manuscript, George Washington University, March 2012, 5 pp. Available at http://www.tspppa.gwu.edu/docs/Fair%20Market%20Values%20and%20the%20Budgetary%20Treatment%20of%20Federal%20Credit%20MP013012Final1.pdf.
[48] Ibid., pp. 1-2.
[49] U.S. Executive Office of the President, Office of Management and Budget, *Analytical Perspectives, Budget of the U.S. Government, Fiscal Year 2013*, U.S. Govt. Print Off., Washington, 2012, pp. 393-399.
[50] Ibid., p. 393.
[51] Ibid., pp. 393-395.
[52] Congressional Budget Office, *Fair-Value Accounting for Federal Credit Programs,* p. 5.
[53] Ibid., p. 10.
[54] Ibid.
[55] Ibid.
[56] Ibid.
[57] Ibid.
[58] Ibid, p. 2.
[59] Ibid.
[60] Ibid., p. 11.
[61] Ibid., p. 5.
[62] Ibid.
[63] This description of Section 507(a) is from the LIS summary written by CRS.

In: Federal Credit
Editor: Ethan A. Kelly

ISBN: 978-1-62417-553-4


*Chapter 3*

# FAIR-VALUE ACCOUNTING FOR FEDERAL CREDIT PROGRAMS*

***Congressional Budget Office***

The federal government supports some private activities—such as home ownership, postsecondary education, and certain commercial ventures—through credit assistance offered to individuals and businesses. Some of that assistance is in the form of direct federal loans, and some is through federal guarantees of loans made by private financial institutions. At the end of fiscal year 2011, about $2.7 trillion was outstanding in such federal direct loans and loan guarantees.[1] The cost of providing credit assistance is an important consideration for policymakers as they allocate spending among programs and choose between credit assistance and other forms of aid such as federal grants—but assessing cost is not a simple matter. Indeed, it is more difficult to measure the cost of credit assistance than to assess the costs of other forms of aid because the measurement of the cost of credit assistance must account for future cash flows of uncertain amounts that can continue for many years.

According to the rules for budgetary accounting prescribed in the Federal Credit Reform Act of 1990 (FCRA, incorporated as title V of the Congressional Budget Act of 1974), the estimated lifetime cost of a new loan or loan guarantee is recorded in the budget in the year in which the loan is disbursed.[2] That lifetime cost is generally described as the subsidy provided by

* This is an edited, reformatted and augmented version of the Congressional Budget Office, dated March 2012.

the loan or loan guarantee. It is measured by discounting all of the expected future cash flows associated with the loan or loan guarantee—including the amounts disbursed, principal repaid, interest received, fees charged, and net losses that accrue from defaults—to a present value at the date the loan is disbursed.

A present value is a single number that expresses a flow of current and future income, or payments, in terms of a lump sum received, or paid, today; the present value depends on the rate of interest, known as the discount rate, that is used to translate future cash flows into current dollars.[3]

FCRA-based cost estimates, however, do not provide a comprehensive measure of what federal credit programs actually cost the government and, by extension, taxpayers.

Under FCRA's rules, the present value of expected future cash flows is calculated by discounting them using the rates on U.S. Treasury securities with similar terms to maturity. Because that procedure does not fully account for the cost of the risk the government takes on when issuing loans or loan guarantees, it makes the reported cost of federal direct loans and loan guarantees in the federal budget lower than the cost that private institutions would assign to similar credit assistance based on market prices. Specifically, private institutions would generally calculate the present value of expected future cash flows by discounting those flows using the rates of return on private loans (or securities) with similar risks and maturities. Because the rates of return on private loans exceed Treasury rates, the discounted value of expected loan repayments is smaller under this alternative approach, which implies a larger cost of issuing a loan. (Similar reasoning implies that the private cost of a loan guarantee would be higher than its cost as estimated under FCRA.)[4]

FCRA and market-based cost estimates alike take into account expected losses from defaults by borrowers. However, because FCRA estimates use Treasury interest rates instead of market-based rates for discounting, FCRA estimates do not incorporate the cost of the market risk associated with the loans.

Market risk is the component of financial risk that remains even after investors have diversified their portfolios as much as possible; it arises from shifts in macroeconomic conditions, such as productivity and employment, and from changes in expectations about future macroeconomic conditions. Loans and loan guarantees expose the government to market risk because future repayments of loans tend to be lower when the economy as a whole is performing poorly and resources are more highly valued.

Some observers argue that using market-based rates for discounting loan repayments to the federal government would be inappropriate because the government can fund its loans by issuing Treasury debt and thus does not seem to pay a price for market risk. However, Treasury rates are lower than those market-based rates primarily because Treasury debt holders are protected against default risk.

If payments from borrowers fall short of what is owed to the federal government, the shortfall must be made up eventually either by raising taxes or by cutting other spending. (Issuing additional Treasury debt can postpone but not avert the need to raise taxes or cut spending.) Therefore, a more comprehensive approach to measuring the cost of federal credit programs would recognize market risk as a cost to the government and would calculate present values using market-based discount rates.

Under such an approach, the federal budget would reflect the market values of loans and loan guarantees.

Accounting for a credit program's budgetary costs using FCRA procedures instead of market values has important consequences for the way policymakers might perceive the cost of credit assistance:

- The costs reported in the budget are generally lower than the costs to even the most efficient private financial institutions for providing credit on the same terms;
- The budgetary costs of federal credit programs are almost always lower than those of other federal spending that imposes equivalent true costs on taxpayers; and
- Purchases of loans at market prices appear to make money for the government and, conversely, sales of loans at market prices appear to result in losses.

What is termed the fair-value approach to budgeting for federal credit programs would measure those programs' costs at market prices or at some approximation of market prices when directly comparable market prices are unavailable.

A fair-value approach generally entails applying the discount rates on expected future cash flows that private financial institutions would apply.[5] In the view of the Congressional Budget Office (CBO), adopting a fair-value approach would provide a more comprehensive way to measure the costs of federal credit programs and would permit more level comparisons between those costs and the costs of other forms of federal assistance.

Several other considerations would be relevant in judging whether to adopt a fair-value approach to federal budgeting. In addition to the practical matters of how to implement and apply a fair-value approach, there are others:

- Government agencies would incur additional expense, for instance, for training staff members in fair-value estimating and for developing new valuation models.
- Fair-value cost estimates would be somewhat more volatile over time because of changes in market conditions—although factors that also affect FCRA estimates would continue to be the main cause of volatility.
- Fair-value estimates require analysts to make judgments about discount rates for each program, which could be an additional source of inconsistency in the estimates of costs from program to program.
- Fair-value estimates also are considered by some observers to be less transparent than FCRA estimates are, and they could be more difficult to communicate to policymakers and the public.

Those final two sets of concerns in particular could be mitigated by relying on expert advice from private-sector accounting firms with significant experience in fair-value accounting or by establishing federal guidelines for estimation procedures.

The government already uses fair-value estimates in budgeting for a few types of programs or transactions, including commitments of resources for some International Monetary Fund lending facilities and the Troubled Asset Relief Program.[6] In addition, CBO uses a fair-value approach to incorporate the budgetary costs of Fannie Mae and Freddie Mac into its budget projections, and the agency has provided supplementary information to the Congress about fair-value estimates for the costs of other federal credit programs (including student loan programs, loan guarantees for nuclear power plant construction, and single-family mortgage guarantees).

In some cases, fair-value estimates of budgetary costs as a percentage of loan amounts are considerably higher than FCRA estimates: CBO has estimated that the average subsidy for direct student loans made between 2010 and 2020 would be a *negative* 9 percent under FCRA accounting but a *positive* 12 percent on a fair-value basis. (A negative subsidy indicates that, for budgetary purposes, the transactions are recorded as generating net income for the government.) Subsequent changes in CBO's interest rate projections would affect both estimates of the amounts of those subsidies, but the large gap between them would remain. In other cases, however, the difference is more modest: For example, CBO has estimated that the cost of the Federal Housing Administration's (FHA's) guarantees of single-family home mortgages to be extended in 2012 would be -1.9 percent on a FCRA basis and 1.5 percent on a fair-value basis.

The federal budget is designed to account for costs to tax-payers but not for the value of government programs to participants or to society more broadly.

Credit assistance, like other federal spending, can increase public well-being by supporting activities that, although beneficial to society, are unlikely to be economically viable without government support. Credit assistance also can have unintended negative consequences, such as encouraging high household debt or creating incentives for overinvestment in certain activities. Although the broader benefits and costs of programs should be considered along with their budgetary costs, the focus in this document is on the best way to measure the costs that appear in the budget.[7]

## FEDERAL CREDIT PROGRAMS

Credit assistance is provided by the federal government in the form of direct loans to borrowers and guarantees of loans made by others. With direct loans, the government collects scheduled interest and repayments of principal (net of amounts not paid when there is a default), and in some cases the government also charges borrowers fees. With guaranteed loans, the government may collect fees at origination and annually from the financial institution or the borrower; in return, the government agrees to cover all or a portion of losses if the borrower defaults. The largest share of federal credit assistance (holding aside that provided by Fannie Mae and Freddie Mac) has come through a few programs. FHA's mortgage guarantees and the Department of Education's student loan programs together accounted for more than two-thirds of federally backed credit outstanding at the end of fiscal year 2011. Other major programs include the Department of Veterans Affairs' mortgage guarantee programs, the Department of Agriculture's credit programs (primarily for rural utilities), and the Small Business Administration's loan and loan guarantee programs. In addition, more than 150 smaller credit programs provide assistance for a variety of activities, including international trade and investments in new technology. From 1992 to 2011, the amount of federal direct loans and federally guaranteed loans outstanding in programs that are recorded in the budget as specified in FCRA grew from $860 billion to about $2.7 trillion (see Table 1). The average growth rate of about 6 percent per year is similar to that for overall federal spending during the period. Guaranteed loans made up about three-quarters of the loans outstanding in 2011, and direct loans accounted for the rest. In the aftermath of the financial crisis of 2007, reliance on federal credit programs accelerated sharply as the supply of private financing contracted and its cost escalated for many borrowers; originations of new federally backed loans spiked above $600 billion in 2009 (see Figure 1). The amount has since declined from that peak, but in 2011 it was still more than double that before the crisis.

An important form of federal credit assistance that is not included in those figures is that of the mortgage guarantees issued by Fannie Mae and Freddie Mac; through those institutions, the federal government now backs roughly half of the $11 trillion in mortgages outstanding in the United States.

**Table 1. Loans and Loan Guarantees in Major Federal Credit Programs**

| | Billions of Dollars of Credit Outstanding | | Annual Percentage Change 1992–2011 | Percentage of Credit Outstanding | |
|---|---|---|---|---|---|
| | **1992** | **2011** | | **1992** | **2011** |
| Federal Housing Administration Programs | 387 | 1,181 | 6 | 45 | 44 |
| Student Loans | 79 | 706 | 12 | 9 | 26 |
| Veterans' Home Loans | 176 | 258 | 2 | 20 | 10 |
| Department of Agriculture Credit Programs | 88 | 99 | 1 | 10 | 4 |
| Small Business Administration Programs | 17 | 82 | 9 | 2 | 3 |
| Other[a] | 113 | 339 | 6 | 13 | 13 |
| **Total** | **860** | **2,665** | **6** | **100** | **100** |

Source: Congressional Budget Office based on data compiled by the Office of Management and Budget.

[a]. Excludes the activities of Fannie Mae and Freddie Mac, purchases by the Treasury of securities issued by Fannie Mae and Freddie Mac, the financial assets acquired through the Troubled Asset Relief Program, and certain other transactions that involve credit assistance but that are generally not considered direct federal loans or loan guarantees.

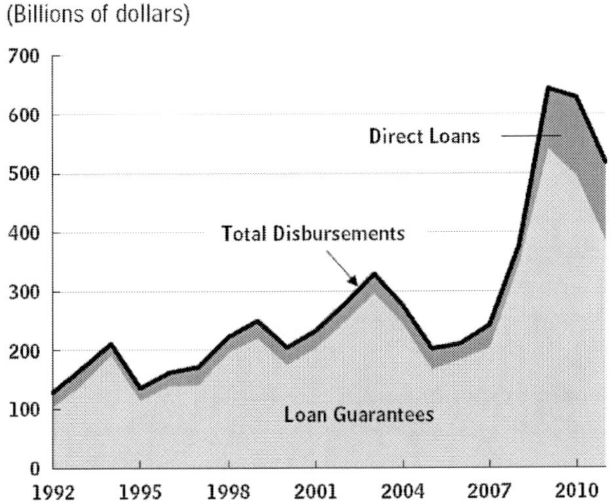


Source: Congressional Budget Office based on data compiled by the Office of Management and Budget.

Note: Excludes the activities of Fannie Mae and Freddie Mac, purchases by the Treasury of securities issued by Fannie Mae and Freddie Mac, the financial assets acquired through the Troubled Asset Relief Program, amounts committed to the International Monetary Fund, the consolidation loans offered by the Department of Education, and certain other transactions that involve credit assistance but that generally are not considered federal direct loans or loan guarantees.

Figure 1. New Federal Direct Loans and Loan Guarantees.

In 2008, the federal government took control of the two entities, and it now operates them to fulfill the public purpose of supporting the residential housing and mortgage markets. Both entities rely on federal backing to maintain their low-cost access to financial markets. Although they are not legally government agencies, and their employees are not civil servants, CBO believes that they are effectively part of the government, so the agency includes the financial transactions of the two entities alongside all other federal activities in its budget projections.

In contrast, the Office of Management and Budget (OMB) treats the entities as nongovernmental and therefore generally reflects only the cash transactions between the Treasury and Fannie Mae and Freddie Mac in the budget. Including the 21 percent of new home loans insured by federal agencies such as FHA and the 63 percent of new home loans insured by Fannie Mae and Freddie Mac, about 84 percent of new mortgages in 2011 carried a federal guarantee.

## BUDGET PROCEDURES PRESCRIBED BY FCRA

FCRA specifies that the subsidy cost of credit is to be calculated and recorded on an accrual basis—unlike most items in the federal budget, which are shown on a cash basis. The main distinction between the two forms of accounting is that under cash accounting, expenditures are recorded in the years that cash payments are made; accrual accounting allows the estimated lifetime cost of a direct loan or loan guarantee to be recognized in the year that the loan is made and, thus, when resources are firmly committed. (A system of supporting accounts is used to reconcile FCRA accruals with the cash flows associated with credit programs.)[8]

One advantage of accounting for credit programs on an accrual basis is that it eliminates the incentive that would exist under cash accounting to favor loan guarantees over economically equivalent direct loans. On a cash basis, a loan guarantee often would appear to be much less expensive than a direct loan with the same default risk because fees are collected when the loan is originated but defaults often occur much later in the life of the loan. In contrast, the initial outlay of principal for a direct loan occurs in the current year, whereas the return of that principal and many of the interest payments may not occur until many years later.

Under FCRA, the subsidy cost of a direct loan or loan guarantee is calculated as a present value of expected net cash flows over the life of the loan; that present value depends on the discount rate that is used to translate future cash flows into current dollars. FCRA subsidy costs are estimated by discounting expected net cash flows to the time of loan disbursement using interest rates on Treasury securities of comparable maturities. For example, cash flows a year after disbursement are discounted using the rate on Treasury securities with one year to maturity, and those five years out are discounted using the five-year Treasury rate. For loan guarantees, expected cash flows include expected payments by the government to cover default or delinquency, offset by any expected payments to the government, including origination or other fees, penalties, and recoveries on defaulted loans. For direct government loans, expected cash flows include loan disbursements and expected repayments of interest and principal (that is, interest and principal payments after defaults, recoveries, and prepayments), fees, and penalties.

The initial estimates of the cost of federal loan guarantee and direct loan programs in each year have historically amounted to a small fraction of the volume of loans disbursed. Subsidy costs averaged $3.1 billion annually for federally backed loans made from 1998 to 2008, for example, representing an average subsidy rate (the subsidy cost divided by the amount disbursed) of 3.3 percent. In 2009 and 2010, total subsidy costs recorded in the budget fell to -$19 billion and -$20 billion, respectively; that is, government credit assistance reduced the budget deficit reported in those years. In 2011, total subsidy costs were even lower, at -$42 billion. The reduced cost is largely attributable to economic, legislative, and administrative changes to student loan and FHA programs. In particular, the reduction in costs (leading to subsidy estimates that are more negative) reflects the widening gap between the rate charged on new federal student loans and Treasury interest rates, legislation that replaced the guaranteed student loan program with direct student loans (for newly originated loans), and increases in fees charged to borrowers by FHA.

## Causes and Consequences of Understating the Cost of Federal Credit Programs

FCRA cost estimates understate the cost of federal credit programs to the government because of the requirement that Treasury rates be used for discounting. Using comprehensive cost measures for budgeting, and accounting for credit on a basis that is equivalent to that for other federal programs—stated objectives of FCRA—would be better accomplished if the cost of extending federal credit was assessed at market prices rather than on a FCRA basis.

The budgetary cost of any program accounted for on an accrual basis—including the credit programs under FCRA—depends not only on expected future cash flows but also on the discount rates chosen to convert those cash flows into present values. For that reason, the budgetary cost of a credit program does not correspond to the actual cash flows associated with the program; rather, the budgetary cost recorded upon the disbursement of a new loan measures the up-front value of federal resources committed to new loans or loan guarantees. Because FCRA accounting uses Treasury rates to discount all expected future cash flows, regardless of risk, the budgetary costs of federal loans and loan guarantees are disconnected from market prices. In particular, FCRA estimates of the subsidy costs of direct loans and loan guarantees generally are lower than the present-value cost that private financial institutions would assign to the same projected future cash flows.

Economists attribute most of the difference between FCRA and market valuations of loans and loan guarantees to investors' requiring compensation—a market risk premium—for the risk associated with such loans and loan guarantees. Macroeconomic conditions affect the value of most assets and liabilities, although to varying degrees. Most investments are more likely to have low returns when the economy as a whole is weak and resources are especially scarce and highly valued and to have high returns in times of relative plenty when resources are less valuable. Such investments are exposed to market risk, and investors require compensation for bearing that risk; the greater the correlation between the returns on the investment and the state of the overall economy, the greater the amount of the risk, and the greater the required compensation. By contrast, investors do not expect to earn a risk premium on investments whose risk can be neutralized if they are held as part of a diversified portfolio.

In effect, the discount rate that investors apply to cash flows for a risky loan is higher than the rate on Treasury securities by the amount of a market risk premium— and the more market risk associated with the loan, the higher the premium. If taxpayers were to finance such a loan as private investors, they would use discount rates that include a market risk premium to estimate the value of the loan, which would have the effect of assigning a higher cost to potential losses than under FCRA accounting. Because FCRA accounting requires the use of Treasury rates for discounting, it implicitly treats the market risk associated with federal credit programs as having no cost to the government. As a result, the subsidy provided by the government is understated under FCRA accounting. Moreover, the higher the market risk that is associated with a credit obligation, the greater is that understatement. (The costs of risk to the federal government and how they compare with such costs to the private sector are discussed further in Box 1.)

Using Treasury discount rates also reduces the comparability of the estimated budgetary cost of credit and the budgetary cost of most of the government's other activities, which is calculated on the basis of market prices. For example, grants or monetary transfers are recorded in the budget at their cash value, and recipients use those funds to purchase goods and services at market prices. Government purchases from the private sector, such as for military hardware, the labor of the federal workforce, buildings, computers, and electricity, also must cover the private cost of providing those resources, including the cost of the capital used to produce them.

One consequence of using Treasury rates to calculate the cost of federal credit assistance is that some large credit programs, such as FHA's mortgage guarantees and the federal direct student loan programs, appear in some years to make money for taxpayers.

## Box 1. What Market Risk Costs the Federal Government and Taxpayers

Loans and loan guarantees generally have significant exposure to so-called market risk because borrowers default on their debt obligations more frequently and with greater severity (meaning that recoveries from the borrowers are lower) when the economy as a whole is weak. Investors require compensation for bearing such risk because losses that occur when the economy is weak are occurring when resources are more highly valued.

Some analysts argue that market risk associated with loans and loan guarantees is much less costly for the federal government than for private investors because of several inherent advantages of the government in extending credit. Specifically, some analysts contend that the federal government is better able to accommodate risk because it can spread risk more widely and because it can borrow money at the Treasury Department's interest rates, which are lower than those in the private sector. In addition, some analysts note that the federal government's costs of extending credit may be lower than the private sector's costs because the government has no obligation to earn a profit on its activities.

In the view of the Congressional Budget Office, those characteristics of the federal government do not alter the basic conclusion that the assumption of market risk represents a cost to the government: When the government extends credit, the associated market risk of those obligations is effectively passed along to citizens who, as investors, would view that risk as costly.

If the federal government is able to spread certain risks more widely than the private sector can, the government may be a relatively efficient provider of certain types of insurance. That is, a private provider of such insurance might charge higher fees if it is unable to transfer the risk to a wide group of investors. However, even if the federal government can spread risks widely, it cannot eliminate the component of risk that is associated with fluctuations in the aggregate economy—market risk—and which investors require compensation to bear.

The federal government's ability to borrow at Treasury rates also does not reduce the cost to taxpayers of the market risk associated with federal credit programs.

Treasury rates are relatively low because the securities are backed by the government's ability to raise taxes. When the government finances a risky loan or loan guarantee by selling a Treasury security, it is effectively shifting risk to members of the public. If such a loan is repaid as expected, the interest and principal payments cover the government's obligation to the holder of the Treasury security, but if the borrower defaults, the obligation to the security holder must be paid for either by raising taxes or by cutting other spending to be able to repay the Treasury debt. (Issuing additional Treasury debt can postpone but not avert the need to raise taxes or cut spending.) Thus, the risk is effectively borne by taxpayers (or by beneficiaries of government programs); like investors, taxpayers and government beneficiaries generally value resources more highly when the economy is performing poorly.

The view that the federal government is a low-cost provider of credit because it does not need to make a profit rests on the notion that the market risk premium represents a type of profit rather than a normal compensation for risk. However, economists view "economic profits" as arising only when the return on private investment exceeds what investors in a competitive market would require. That is, an economic profit is earned when the expected return more than compensates investors for the fact that money in hand now is worth more than the same amount received in the future and for bearing market risk. So, for instance, when a business has a monopoly over a product, it can set prices above costs to earn an economic profit. In competitive financial markets, the presence of many buyers and sellers of financial assets tends to eliminate economic profits, and the risk premium that remains is normal compensation for bearing the risk.

Thus, none of the differences between the federal government and private investors changes the fact that investments with returns that are correlated with the performance of the economy as a whole are risky in a way that other investments are not. Federal credit programs expose taxpayers to that market risk.

That appearance creates a budgetary incentive to expand the programs beyond the scale that would be chosen if the budget reflected their costs at market value. If, instead, the discount rates used in calculating the present values of cash flows for those loans included a market risk premium, estimates for those programs might show a net cost for taxpayers.

In the case of certain other credit programs, the federal government sets interest rates and fees to eliminate the budgetary cost. Because the cost of market risk is not considered in FCRA-based estimates, the government offers credit to borrowers on terms that are generally more favorable than would be offered by even the most efficient and competitive private financial institutions. When the government is not truly more efficient than the private sector at providing credit, those more favorable terms constitute an unrecognized subsidy to borrowers and a hidden cost to the government.

Even when a credit program has a budgetary cost under FCRA, neglecting the market price of risk lowers the reported cost relative to that of a grant or benefit payment with the same market cost, thus skewing the information that policymakers receive. For example, the government could provide assistance to low-income homebuyers through grants that cover down payments or through loan guarantees that subsidize their borrowing. FCRA accounting makes a loan program appear less costly than a grant program with the same cost measured at market value.

The information supplied by FCRA accounting also could mislead policymakers about the merits of buying, selling, or holding loans. Under FCRA, selling a loan at a competitive price in the open market would produce an estimated budgetary loss because the proceeds of the sale would be less than the value the government assigns to carrying the loan, even though the transaction would entail no economic gain or loss (apart from possible indirect effects that would occur as a result of the sale). Conversely, the purchase of a loan at a market price would show a budgetary gain. For example, OMB reported a budgetary gain of almost $6 billion in 2009 for the Treasury's purchases at market prices of mortgage-backed securities issued by Fannie Mae and Freddie Mac.[9]

## THE ALTERNATIVE OF FAIR-VALUE ACCOUNTING

Fair-value accounting is an alternative to FCRA accounting that more fully incorporates the cost to the government (and, by extension, taxpayers) of the risks inherent in federal credit transactions. The fair-value approach produces estimates of the cost of providing credit that either correspond to or approximate the market price of that credit. Thus, moving to fair-value accounting would provide policymakers, program administrators, and the public with a more complete picture of program costs, and it would tend to make purchases and sales of loans at market prices by federal agencies budget-neutral. It also would put credit on a more level playing field with most other federal expenditures. However, the Congress and federal agencies would confront several challenges in adopting fair-value accounting, including the expense of implementing a new system and the need to cope with the greater difficulty—especially initially—of estimating, verifying, and communicating program costs.[10]

## Fair-Value Accounting

The fair value of a loan is the price that would be received if the loan were sold in what is known as an orderly transaction—one that occurs under competitive market conditions between willing participants and that does not involve forced liquidation or a distressed sale.[11] Similarly, the fair value of a loan guarantee is the price that would have to be paid to induce a private financial institution to assume the guarantee commitment. FCRA-based and fair-value estimates alike incorporate the same projections of future cash flows. But instead of using Treasury rates to discount those cash flows, fair-value estimates employ discounting methods that are consistent with the risk of the loan or loan guarantee. (See Box 2 for a numerical example of subsidy cost calculations under FCRA and fair-value accounting.) One consequence of switching to fair-value accounting is that the reported budgetary costs of most direct loan and loan guarantee programs would be higher than they appear under FCRA accounting: Credit programs that show modest budgetary savings or that have a subsidy cost of zero under FCRA would tend to show a positive subsidy with fair-value accounting, and programs that have positive subsidies now would see that subsidy rate increase. For instance, a program that offers loans to borrowers at or just slightly above Treasury rates and that has a low average default rate would show a positive fair-value subsidy cost because of the market risk that those loans entail.

## Concerns about Implementation

Fair values for government loans and loan guarantees can be estimated by reference to the market prices of similar products offered by private companies (for example, the interest rates charged on private-sector loans to students can be combined with other information to infer a risk premium for federal student loans) or by employing standard financial valuation techniques (such as discounting expected cash flows with risk-adjusted discount rates, or using an options-pricing model—a type of model that many private-sector practitioners use to evaluate guarantees).

## BOX 2. COMPARISON OF METHODS: FCRA AND FAIR-VALUE ACCOUNTING

### FCRA and Fair-Value Treatments of a Three-Year Direct Loan for $100 Million at 3 Percent Interest

| (Millions of dollars) | | | | | |
|---|---|---|---|---|---|
| | Year | | | | Subsidy[a] |
| | 0 | 1 | 2 | 3 | |
| | Cash Flows | | | | |
| Disbursement | 100 | 0 | 0 | 0 | n.a. |
| Scheduled Interest Payments | 0 | -3 | -2 | -1 | n.a. |
| Scheduled Principal Payments | 0 | -33 | -33 | -34 | n.a. |
| Default Losses | 0 | 1 | 1 | 1 | n.a. |
| Net Cash Outflow from the Federal Government | 100 | -35 | -34 | -34 | n.a. |
| | FCRA Treatment | | | | |
| Treasury Discount Rate (Percent per annum) | 0 | 0.25 | 0.50 | 1.00 | n.a. |
| FCRA Present-Value Factor b | 1 | 0.998 | 0.990 | 0.971 | n.a. |
| FCRA Discounted Net Cash Outflow from the Federal Government[c] | 100 | -34.9 | -33.7 | -33.0 | -1.6 |
| | Fair-Value Treatment | | | | |
| Fair-Value Discount Rate (Percent per annum) | 0 | 1.75 | 2.00 | 2.50 | n.a. |
| Fair-Value Present-Value Factor[b] | 1 | 0.983 | 0.961 | 0.929 | n.a. |
| Fair-Value Discounted Net Cash Outflow from the Federal Government[c] | 100 | -34.4 | -32.7 | -31.6 | 1.3 |

Source: Congressional Budget Office.

Note: FCRA = Federal Credit Reform Act of 1990; n.a. = not applicable.

a. Sum of the discounted net cash outflow.

b. One divided by (one plus the discount rate) raised to the power of the number of years until the payment is made or received. For example, $1/(1 + 0.5/100)^2 = 0.990$.

c. The net cash outflow multiplied by the present-value factor.

Consider a $100 million portfolio of federal direct loans with 3-year terms and an annual interest rate of 3 percent. Net federal cash flows each year include disbursements, the scheduled payments of principal and interest, and default losses (see the table). Note that the net interest and principal payments that the government will receive are the scheduled payments of principal and interest minus the amounts that are expected not to be paid by or recovered from the borrowers because of default.

According to the rules for budgetary accounting prescribed in the Federal Credit Reform Act of 1990 (FCRA, incorporated as title V of the Congressional Budget Act of 1974), the net cash flow in each future year is discounted at a compounded annual rate equal to the yield on Treasury securities with the same term to maturity—up to three years, in the current example.[1] The FCRA subsidy of -$1.6 million (that is, a net reduction in the budget deficit) is the sum across all years of the net cash outflow from the government in each year discounted on a FCRA basis (that is, the annual net cash outflow multiplied by the corresponding present-value factor).

Suppose that, on the basis of observed pricing for a privately held portfolio that is comparable to the federal loan portfolio, the implied fair-value discount rate for the cash flows in each period is 1.5 percentage points higher than the corresponding Treasury rate. The fair-value subsidy is computed in the same way as the FCRA subsidy, using the same net cash outflows, but the present-value factor is computed from the Treasury rate plus the market risk premium of 1.5 percentage points. Accounting for market risk in this example changes the estimated subsidy to a positive subsidy of $1.3 million, which implies a cost to the government.

1. Section 502(5)(E) of FCRA, 2 U.S.C. §661a (5)(E) (2006).

CBO has applied each of those methods in various analyses of credit programs; the choice of methodology has depended on which approach was expected to produce the most reliable estimates given the characteristics of the obligations being evaluated and the information available.[12]

In private-sector applications (such as in financial reporting by large financial institutions), fair values are based on actual market prices whenever reliable prices are available. However, when comparable credit products are not publicly traded—or during a financial crisis, when the few transactions that occur are likely to be at distressed prices—fair values must be approximated. Because most public-sector credit programs have no exact analogue in the private sector, estimating their fair value usually involves approximation. In addition, adjustments may be needed to account for true cost differences between the government and the private sector; for instance, the private sector generally spends more than the government does on marketing. Private lenders would set interest rates and fees to recover those higher costs, and if the difference was not accounted for, the cost of the federal program would be overstated. Implementing fair-value accounting for federal credit programs would entail additional effort and expense for government agencies, particularly OMB, which oversees the process of estimating the costs of such programs. Start-up expenses of the fair-value approach would include funding for additional training and possible expansion of staff, redesign of procedures and account structures, and development of models and approaches for producing the estimates. Even over the long term, some additional resources would probably be needed because of the estimates' greater complexity. Failure to provide the necessary funding, both for start-up costs and for the continuing costs of a switch to fair-value accounting, could leave the government and policymakers with insufficient information for making choices about future federal credit assistance.

Incorporating the cost of market risk into budgetary cost estimates for credit programs also would tend to increase those estimates' volatility over time because the cost of market risk is not constant. However, the additional volatility introduced would probably be less than the considerable volatility of FCRA estimates that is attributable to fluctuating Treasury rates, swings in projected losses resulting from defaults, and administrative changes in fees and other terms of loans. For example, the fair-value estimates of costs for the Troubled Asset Relief Program have changed considerably over time, but those changes are primarily the result of changes in the components of the estimates that also would have been used in FCRA estimates, such as projections of participation rates in government programs and projections of the repayment rates of loans.

Another concern is that fair-value estimates might be less transparent than FCRA estimates and thus more dependent on the judgment of agencies and analysts responsible for the programs, creating inconsistencies among programs and making estimates more difficult to communicate to policymakers or the public.

FCRA and fair-value estimates alike depend on analysts' projections of such variables as prepayment patterns, default rates, and the amounts recoverable after a default. The models that agencies use to project cash flows generally are not made public now, so the transparency of current FCRA estimates is limited. However, fair-value estimates would be even more dependent on analysts' judgment because they would depend on choices about market risk premiums in addition to estimates of cash flows.

Such concerns could be addressed in various ways—for example, through the use of accounting practices similar to those used to audit fair-value estimates produced by private financial institutions. Guidelines also could be established by OMB or through legislation to ensure that the choices of discount rates and other assumptions that are used in the models followed systematic procedures and could be adequately verified. Briefing sessions for the staff of the Congress and federal agencies as well as development of materials that explained how the estimates were derived would facilitate communication about the estimates.

## Accounting for Administrative Costs

FCRA accounting separates the administrative expenses of federal credit programs from the programs' subsidy costs, and it accounts for administrative expenses on a cash basis. The consequent mix of cash and accrual accounting, and the use of multiple accounts, makes assessing the total costs of a program difficult. It also complicates cost comparisons from one program to another.

Comprehensive fair-value estimates of subsidies for credit programs would incorporate certain administrative expenses, such as servicing and collection costs, that are essential to preserving the value of the government's claims (rather than accounting separately for those costs on a cash basis). Those essential preservation expenses can differ significantly among credit programs, and including them in subsidy cost estimates would make comparing various subsidy costs easier. However, doing so could erode Congressional control over program expenditures because, under FCRA, all increases in estimated costs after a loan or loan guarantee is initiated (including those arising from increased expenditures on servicing or loan collection) are automatically appropriated.[13]

Another concern is that implementing a switch from cash to accrual accounting for essential preservation expenses would be administratively complicated.

Moreover, although including administrative costs in subsidy estimates would improve comparability between different credit programs, in some instances it might hinder the ability to compare credit assistance and grant programs.

Grant programs also incur administrative costs, and those costs are not readily linked to the funds disbursed in any one year. Including all administrative costs in credit programs but not in grant programs could reduce comparability between the two. However, if the adjustment was just for essential preservation expenses in credit programs, comparability with grant costs could be improved because grant recipients generally do not need to repay the government in future years and hence there are few preservation expenses associated with most grants.

# COMPARING FCRA AND FAIR-VALUE COSTS FOR SELECTED FEDERAL CREDIT PROGRAMS

In a few cases, the law has required the use of fair-value accounting in the federal budget process: The law that created the Troubled Asset Relief Program, for example, specifies the use of a fair-value approach.[14] A different law requires that funds committed to certain International Monetary Fund lending facilities receive fair-value treatment.[15] In addition, CBO has used a fair-value approach to incorporate the costs of Fannie Mae and Freddie Mac into its baseline budget projections since those companies were placed into federal conservatorship.[16]

CBO also has provided supplementary information to the Congress about the fair-value costs of certain federal credit and insurance programs and how those costs compare with FCRA-based costs. Several years ago, for example, the agency provided fair-value estimates for the Small Business Administration's 7(a) program and for activities of the Pension Benefit Guaranty Corporation, among others.[17] Most recently, CBO has prepared fair-value estimates for the federal direct and guaranteed student loan programs, the Department of Energy's program to guarantee loans for the construction of nuclear power plants, and the Federal Housing Administration's single-family mortgage insurance program.

## Student Loans

In 2011, the total amount outstanding for federal direct and guaranteed student loans exceeded $700 billion. Federal student loans expose the government to losses from defaults, and they involve significant administrative expenses for origination, servicing, and collection on defaults; at the same time, the government collects fees and interest from borrowers. As with other types of credit, student loans are exposed to market risk, meaning that default rates tend to be higher, and recoveries smaller, when the economy is weak and the losses are most costly.

CBO compared the cost of the federal student loan programs on a FCRA versus a fair-value basis in a 2010 study.[18] CBO calculated that, on average over the 2010–2020 period, a representative loan issued in the direct student loan program would have a negative subsidy rate of 9 percent under FCRA (thereby reducing the deficit) but a positive subsidy rate of 12 percent on a fair-value basis.

## Loan Guarantees for Nuclear Power Plant Construction

The Energy Policy Act of 2005 established incentives to encourage private investment in new technology, including advanced nuclear energy facilities.[19] In return for a loan guarantee, the Department of Energy can charge project sponsors a fee to recoup the guarantee's estimated budgetary cost, which, on a FCRA basis, is likely to be well below the fair-value cost. To date no loans have been guaranteed under the program, although there are several active applications.

CBO has estimated the costs of guarantees for nuclear power plant construction using projects' credit ratings to derive expected default rates and risk-adjusted discount rates.[20] In all cases, the estimated subsidy rate was significantly higher on a fair-value basis than on a FCRA basis, but the difference between the subsidy rates varied widely with a project's credit rating and the amounts expected to be recovered in the event of a default. If the risk associated with a guaranteed loan for plant construction was in the range of risks posed by bonds rated A (less risky) and bonds rated BB (riskier), then CBO's estimate of the budgetary cost on a FCRA basis ranged from 1 percent to 6 percent of the loan's principal amount. In contrast, under the same circumstances, CBO's estimate of the budgetary cost on a fair-value basis ranged from 9 percent to 21 percent of the loan's principal.

## FHA's Single-Family Mortgage Guarantees

FHA's single-family mortgage insurance program is aimed at extending access to home ownership to people who lack the savings, credit history, or income to qualify for a conventional mortgage. Under FHA's program, the government insures 15- and 30-year fixed- and adjustable-rate mortgages for home purchases or for refinancing; in exchange, the borrower pays an origination fee and annual premiums on the insurance policy. In 2011, the outstanding stock of single-family mortgage guarantees insured by FHA totaled almost $1.2 trillion.

CBO has compared the FCRA and fair-value costs projected for FHA's single-family program in 2012, which CBO estimated would guarantee $233 billion in mortgages. To compute the fair value of the guarantees, CBO relied primarily on the market pricing of private mortgage insurance and on estimates of the fair value of the mortgage guarantees made by Fannie Mae and Freddie Mac.[21] Under FCRA accounting, CBO estimated a negative subsidy rate for FHA single-family home loan guarantees of 1.9 percent, producing budgetary savings of $4.4 billion in 2012. On a fair-value basis, however, CBO estimated that those guarantees would have a positive subsidy rate of 1.5 percent, and the program would have a cost of $3.5 billion.

## End Notes

[1] The figures for federal credit outstanding and new lending activity cited in this document exclude the activities of Fannie Mae and Freddie Mac, even though the government placed the two entities into conservatorship in 2008 (as discussed later). The figures also exclude purchases by the Treasury of securities issued by Fannie Mae and Freddie Mac, the financial assets acquired through the Troubled Asset Relief Program, amounts committed to the Inter-national Monetary Fund, and certain other transactions that involve credit assistance but that generally are not considered direct federal loans or loan guarantees. Consolidation loans offered by the Department of Education are counted toward credit outstanding but excluded from new lending activity because the Congressional Budget Office considers those loans extensions of the original loans.

[2] Section 504(d) of FCRA, 2 U.S.C. § 661c (d) (2006).

[3] For example, if an investment that will yield $100 one year in the future is discounted at 5 percent, its value today is $95.

[4] See Congressional Budget Office, Federal Loan Guarantees for the HYPERLINK "http://www.cbo.gov/publication/41510"Construction of Nuclear Power Plants, Appendix C (August 2011).

[5] In some cases fair values are calculated by using risk-adjusted discount rates, but in other cases fair values are more accurately estimated using other standard techniques, such as options-pricing models.

[6] On February 7, 2012, the House of Representatives passed the Budget and Accounting Transparency Act of 2012 (H.R. 3581, 112th Cong., 2nd Sess.), which would expand the use of fair-value accounting in the budget.

[7] Some analysts have argued that it may be appropriate to include the full costs of risk to taxpayers in cost–benefit analyses but not in budget estimates because the costs of risk do not represent an actual government cost (see, for example, Jim Horney, Richard Kogan, and Paul Van de Water, House Bill Would Artificially Inflate Cost of Federal Credit Programs [Washington, D.C.: Center on Budget and Policy Priorities], January 2012). For the reasons laid out in this document, CBO's view is that the cost of risk is a real cost to the government that is relevant for budgeting as well as for cost–benefit analyses. (For a detailed response to Horney and others, see Marvin Phaup, "Fair Market Values and the Budgetary Treatment of Federal Credit: Comment on CBPP's Release on H.R. 3581," manuscript, George Washington University, www.tspppa.gwu.edu/docs/Fair%20Market%20Values%20and%20the%20Budgetary%20Treatment%20of%20Federal%20HYPERLINK "http://www.tspppa.gwu.edu/docs/Fair Market Values and the Budgetary Treatment of Federal Credit MP013012Final1.pdf"Credit%20MP013012Final1.pdf.)

[8] See Office of Management and Budget, Circular A-11 (2011), Part 5: Federal Credit, www. whitehouse.gov/omb/circulars_ HYPERLINK "http://www.whitehouse.gov/omb/ circulars_a11_current_year_a11_toc"a11_current_year_a11_toc.

[9] See Budget of the United States Government, Fiscal Year 2010, Analytical Perspectives, p. 76, Table 7-9, www.gpo.gov/fdsys/pkg/HYPERLINK "http://www.gpo.gov/fdsys/ pkg/BUDGET-2010-PER/content-detail.html"BUDGET-2010-PER/content-detail.html. Loan purchases and sales by Fannie Mae and Freddie Mac do not have a direct effect on the federal budget, which generally only reflects cash trans-actions between the Treasury and those entities. However, the Treasury's purchases of mortgage-backed securities were accounted for on a FCRA basis, a departure from cash treatment.

[10] See "Special Topics," Budget of the United States Government, Fiscal Year 2013, Analytical Perspectives, pp. 373–379, www.whitehouse.gov/omb/budget/Analytical_Perspectives.

[11] See Financial Accounting Standards Board, Original Pronouncements, as Amended. Statement of Financial Accounting Standards No. 157: Fair Value Measurements (Norwalk, Conn.: Financial Accounting Foundation, 2010), www.fasb.org/pdf/aop_FAS157.pdf.

[12] For additional information on alternative approaches to calculating the fair value of federal credit programs, see Deborah Lucas and Marvin Phaup, "The Cost of Risk to the Government and Its Implications for Federal Budgeting," in Deborah Lucas, ed., Measuring and Managing Federal Financial Risk (University of Chicago Press, 2010), pp. 29–54.

[13] Section 504(f) of FCRA, 2 U.S.C. §661c (f) (2006).

[14] In particular, the legislation stated that the estimated cost of the program's obligations must be recorded in the budget on a FCRA basis rather than a cash basis but that the discount rate must be adjusted for the market cost of risk. (See section 123 of the Emergency Economic Stabilization Act of 2008, Division A of Public Law 110-343, 122 Stat. 3765, 3790.)

[15] Title XIV of the Supplemental Appropriations Act, 2009, P.L.111-32, 123 Stat. 1859, 1916.

[16] See Congressional Budget Office, CBO's Budgetary Treatment of HYPERLINK "http://www.cbo.gov/doc.cfm?index=10878"Fannie Mae and Freddie Mac , Background Paper (January 2010).

[17] See Congressional Budget Office, Federal Financial Guarantees HYPERLINK "http://www.cbo.gov/ftpdocs/87xx/doc8708/10-15-SBA.pdf"Under the Small Business Administration's 7(a) Program (October 2007); The Risk Exposure of the Pension Benefit Guaranty CorporaHYPERLINK "http://www.cbo.gov/ftpdocs/66xx/doc6646/09-15-PBGC.pdf"tion (September 2005); and Estimating the Value of Subsidies for HYPERLINK "http://www.cbo.gov/doc.cfm?index=5751"Federal Loans and Loan Guarantees (August 2004).

[18] See Congressional Budget Office, Costs and Policy Options for HYPERLINK "http://www.cbo.gov/doc.cfm?index=11043"Federal Student Loan Programs (March 2010); and the letter to the HYPERLINK "http://www.cbo.gov/doc.cfm?index=11343"Honorable Judd Gregg about the budgetary impact of the PresiHYPERLINK "http://www.cbo.gov/ doc.cfm?index=11343"dent's proposal to alter federal student loan programs (March 15, 2010).

[19] Title XVII of the Energy Policy Act of 2005, 42 U.S.C. §16511– 16516 (2006 & Supp.).

[20] See Congressional Budget Office, Federal Loan Guarantees for the HYPERLINK "http://www.cbo.gov/doc.cfm?index=12238"Construction of Nuclear Power Plants. CBO did not analyze any specific projects. As of April 2011, the Department of Energy, which administers the program, had received 19 applications for loan guarantees on $188 billion of debt for the construction of 14 nuclear power plants. Of that number, only one application has been reported to be close to completion.

[21] In the market for private mortgage insurance (PMI), competing private insurers publicly quote prices for guarantees of mortgages that are comparable (after some adjustments) with those guaranteed by FHA. FHA absorbs all of the losses on the mortgages it insures, whereas on mortgages covered by PMI, the mortgage insurers cover losses up to some maximum and the remaining losses are covered by Fannie Mae and Freddie Mac. Therefore, the fair value

of FHA insurance can be inferred from the sum of the value of the PMI premiums and the fair value of premiums charged by Fannie Mae and Freddie Mac. See Congressional Budget Office, "Accounting for FHA's Single-Family Mortgage HYPERLINK "http://www.cbo.gov/doc.cfm?index=12054"Insurance Program on a Fair-Value Basis," attachment to a letter HYPERLINK "http://www.cbo.gov/doc.cfm?index=12054"to the Honorable Paul Ryan (May 18, 2011).

# INDEX

## A



## B



## C

**D**



**E**



**F**

**G**



**H**



**I**